Exploitation, Extortion, Exoneration

A good story is comprised of contrast—extreme contrast—and there is no greater yin versus yang than life or death. —Al Quinn

A Shot in the Texas Dark
An Al Quinn Novel
Russ Hall

REDA DEPT PUBLISHING
Unlocking New Worlds

A Shot in the Texas Dark
An Al Quinn™ Novel
A Red Adept Publishing Book
Red Adept Publishing, LLC
104 Bugenfield Court
Garner, NC 27529
http://RedAdeptPublishing.com/

Chapter One

Al Quinn realized he was gripping his binoculars a little too tightly. He glanced over at Fergie, expecting her to be heating up until she was boiling and bubbling like a coffee percolator. He wasn't wrong.

She spoke through clenched teeth. "You see a brilliant white flash from behind the edges of a drawn motel blind, then another and another, and you just know what that's about. Someone's daughter or sister is having pictures taken that aren't going to make it into a high-school yearbook. She'll be disrobing in stages until she lies back naked before the camera and the eyes of thousands of men made lonely by being single or even by being married."

Al couldn't hear her teeth grind, but he'd heard her on the subject before, and the edge she gave her words hadn't dulled a bit.

"What's especially sad," she said, "is that jobs like the ones you and I retired from rob us of anything like insight or epiphany on stuff like this."

She was a retired city detective. He'd done his detective work for the sheriff's department.

She sighed. "But I suppose we most certainly get plenty of opportunities to feel anything from shame to a slice of humble pie."

Al couldn't think of anything to say to that. He looked back toward the motel. The white camera flashes kept popping, snapping at Al just as the Bone Lady's eyes had earlier in the day, eyes as black as unlit coal yet still able to throw sparks enough for the hottest of fires.

?

As recently as twelve hours before, he had been staring back into those eyes, so intensely black he could see no iris or pupil, just two dark glittering mirrors in which he could imagine tiny reflections of himself.

3

"I want you to find Gerta and make her stop," she said.

"Stop what?"

The Bone Lady glanced toward Fergie, who stood taller than Al and a foot taller than herself. Al had heard from the Cheyenne gal after she had gotten a nudging from her friends, some Native American tribespeople he'd helped in the past as a sheriff's department detective in his years of restless tumbling back and forth from one end of the county to the other. He'd always gone out of his way for such folks, and they seemed to know he'd retired and had time on his hands if someone really needed his help.

Al and Fergie stood in the Bone Lady's place of work. She was covered in the red and drying brown of blood, a knife hanging loosely in one hand with the same casual certainty that a master carpenter had when he held a hammer. Her hairnet matched her apron, which would have been white had it not been splashed with those Jackson Pollock sprays of blood.

Behind her, in glass cases, lay chops, ribs, steaks, and the usual bits of domestic carrion. The building around them was vast, but Al fancied he could hear a distant drip somewhere. Because of the sort of place it was, he wondered if that drip might also be blood.

Al wasn't surprised a woman of her pure blood could do a job like that. After all, the women in the tribes did most of the meat preparation when they weren't gathering firewood or water or handling the heavy lifting for any moves the tribe made. The men needed to make sure the meat kept coming in for the women to prepare.

She answered Al but continued to stare up at Fergie. "Making a fool of herself with some white man."

She raised her other hand from her side, holding the wooden handle of a steel knife. Waiting for Al to speak, she ran the edge of the long knife against the grain of the steel. Al felt the short hairs on his neck rise, not sensing a whole lot of difference between her words and the sound of the honed blade rasping along the steel's edge.

"I have a pretty full plate right now." Al didn't dare glance toward Fergie.

"Look, you don't wanna work for me, you just say so. You've no reason to lie to me." Her sideways-teardrop-shaped eyes narrowed further. She had high cheekbones with the reddish tint he expected from a full-blood.

"It's no lie. I have other active cases right now. And I'm supposed to be retired. I didn't say no. I'm just letting you know how busy I am."

"Ain't none of us restin' on our heels." She nodded toward the back of the shop, where a saw shifted to a higher whine as it moved from cutting meat to cutting bone. "I've got two black-tail deer back there need dressed out 'fore noon."

When Al didn't respond or dare look in Fergie's direction, the Bone Lady said, "Oh, I know all about you. I hear you're likely to leap at cases that have anything to do with prejudice. You think I'm just backed up full of hate?"

Al didn't know what to think. Most people wouldn't accuse him of talking too much, though it had been said he sometimes had a smart mouth when he did open his yap. He was still wrestling with what she'd said when someone called her name from the back room.

"Just a minute," she called back over her shoulder. She lowered the knife and steel, which Al was glad for. "What about it? Can you help me find her?"

"Where is she?"

"I don' know. Why you think I'm buggin' *you*?"

?

A mother trying to find her daughter... that was a whole other thing. That was a worry he could understand, which was how he and Fergie came much, much later to be parked in the lot of a thirty-dollar-a-night flophouse like the Vacationland Motel at going on 3:00 a.m. The buildings, refurbished and salvaged many times, had a deep, rich history, probably of far more sadness than joy. Few families stopped by to stay there, and if they did, they didn't choose to do so again.

"These other cases you mentioned," Fergie said. "Were you referring to me, Maury, and Bonnie?"

"Yeah. You three *are* a handful." Al cleared his throat. "One thing I didn't tell you. This Gerta is fifteen. Her taking off with her mother's car without permission is one thing, a felony if pressed. But if she's inside that motel room, that's a whole other thing."

Fergie's head snapped toward him. "Oh, Al."

"I hate to bug the man at this hour, but I'm going to have to give Victor Kahlon a ring." He dug for his cell phone.

"You might want to give that a second thought or two, Speedy Gonzalez. He's just a detective for the sheriff's department like you were. Even though he's your friend now, this needs to be checked before it's reported, or you're both going to end up wearing an unpleasant aroma. I do think you've got to do something if she is inside that motel room. Are you sure that's her in there? What if it isn't?"

"Well, we don't have anything like a warrant."

"When has that ever stopped you?"

"That sort of thing slowed me down plenty back when I had to follow the book on procedures."

"But you've said it yourself. You're retired."

"They could still drum up a B and E or something against us."

"You're creative. Give it a thought or two."

"Well, we know that's her mother's vehicle." Al nodded toward an olive-green Jeep Cherokee. "And she got here driving it on her learner's permit."

"The DMV said she did the usual driver's ed course at fourteen. She's fifteen now, with a learner's permit. She won't be eligible for a regular driver's license until she's eighteen or for a provisional license until she's sixteen. That would allow her to drive solo but not between midnight and five a.m."

"I know the law, Fergie. I'm old enough to remember back when we called a learner's permit a 'hardship license' so farmers and ranchers could better exploit their kids."

"Then use what you can of the law. How would it apply?"

"At the very least, we probably have suspicion of statutory rape. Or, if there's no sex going on, they could be contributing. She's a minor."

"There you go."

"We're not certain to the bone that it's her in there. What if someone else drove the family car here?"

"You think the Bone Lady herself is in there?"

"No, or we wouldn't still be seeing flashes. She'd be making cutlets out of whoever is using that camera."

"If your reluctance to call Kahlon is because he's a county detective, you might go with one or two of the FBI folks with whom you've worked. You can't use your ICE buddy Jaime Avila. This has nothing to do with immigration. Hell, because of their Native American blood, they might want *us* deported."

"This is county jurisdiction. We could call someone we know on the Child Exploitation Unit that works out of the state attorney general's office. But if it turns out to be some thirty-year-old housewife in there, we would be paddleless up a creek with egg on our faces, to mix up that metaphor and pop it in the blender."

"Sounds like you need more data, Sherlock. You could always call your buddy Sheriff Clayton if you find anything. He's used to bailing you out if you do something stupid. If it's a false alarm, we can just take off and hope they either can't identify us or don't want to file any kind of charges."

Al stared ahead at the flashes coming from the room.

"Or we could just sit here," Fergie said. "I've seen the progression before. You start with a girl so young she exudes a nerdy innocence, just what these pervs want. After way too short a time, she's wearing bright lipstick and too much eye shadow, and she has the look of someone who knows way more about the world than she should at her age."

"Well, hell. We can't just sit here. Let's go do something... possibly illegal... and see how this shakes out." Al reached into the glove box and took out his Sig Sauer, checked it to ensure it was loaded, and slid it inside his belt at the small of his back as he got out of his truck. Fergie was already out her side of the truck. She bent to pull a small Chief's Special from an ankle holster. It wasn't her usual Glock, but it could pack a punch in very close quarters, which seemed likely.

"Why don't you stay in the truck," he said.

"Yeah, like that's gonna happen."

They took slow, soft steps across the gravel to avoid making crunching sounds, although whoever was in that motel room was probably making enough of a racket to drown out any noise outside.

They reached the ice machine at the end of the row of rooms. They walked past the doors until they were outside the right one.

Fergie tapped his shoulder, and he bent close.

"That door looks too tough to kick in," she said. "That's metal on metal. You don't have a lock-pick set in your pocket, do you?"

"Something just as good. Wait here." He eased away.

Barely five minutes later, he came back, easing his way along the row of doors. Fergie leaned around Al to see the fellow he was towing along by his shirt front, a guy who looked pretty much as unenthusiastic as possible. He was making Al drag him, but he wasn't big enough to get away from Al's grip and make a break for it. He was wearing a short-sleeved white shirt that had taken on a yellowish tinge, and not from the mercury vapor lights, either. Half a foot shorter than Al's five-ten, he seemed thin enough that a brisk wind might lift him like a kite.

"Who's that?" Fergie nodded toward the man.

"An old friend with a past, and not a pretty one." Al nodded to the door. "Open it, Bernie."

Whatever Bernie was going to say, possibly something about a warrant, got lost as he swallowed nervously. He stepped closer, took out a master key, and used it on the door's lock.

"Hang onto him. He's apt to make a dash for it." Al twisted the doorknob and charged into the room.

Bernie glanced up at all six-foot-two of Fergie as she reached for him, and he seemed to shrink an inch shorter. He didn't try to shake loose her grip on his upper arm as she tugged him along with them.

Inside the room, all the lights were on. Where the shades could be tilted, they aimed light at the bed. One man was standing behind a camcorder on a tripod and holding the flashing camera with his other hand. His head snapped up toward Al then to the door blocked by Fergie. He looked at the pulled drapes of the windows, perhaps weighing whether he could get to them and through them—probably not. Then he focused on the gun in Al's hand.

The extremely pale naked girl on the bed reached for the bedspread, which lay in a crumpled pile on the floor. She pulled it up and over herself. Al didn't think she looked even fifteen.

Her costar stood upright in his Viagra-enhanced state, looking for something he could drape over himself. He didn't look embarrassed but confused, irritated, and... interrupted.

A guy who had been leaning against the wall to the right decided to make a break for the door. He slid to an abrupt stop with his nose an inch or two away from the barrel of Fergie's Smith & Wesson. She didn't let go of Bernie, who struggled to pull loose from her other hand.

The cameraman leaped at the distraction. He dropped the flash camera onto the bed and ran directly toward Al, who spun and kicked for the uprights, which in this case was the fork in the guy's pants. The cameraman folded into a crumpled tangle on the rug.

"Gerta, get your clothes on," Al said.

The girl was already tugging on her tight jean shorts. Her head spun toward Al. "But I'm not Gerta."

Chapter Two

Al got ushered into Sheriff Clayton's office at ten the next morning, following a deputy who looked far too young for the job, yet another sign that the years were reeling by.

He'd been in that office hundreds of times but nodded at the old, scarred mahogany desk, the row of locked file cabinets along one wall, and the two wood-paneled walls of awards and photo moments with every dignitary, celebrity, and politician in the county. He was as unimpressed as usual. He liked Clayton but doubted he, himself, would ever have been able to play the smiling-handshake game of being sheriff. Al felt a wave of relief once again for having retired when he did.

"Grab a chair, Al." Clayton waved a hand.

Al took in the fellow seated in the other chair across from Clayton. He was the cameraman.

"I'd like to introduce you to Special Agent Aaron Masterson, who, by the way, spent the night with an ice pack on his hacky sack because of you."

Aaron's face flushed red. He half stood and pointed at Al. "I want this guy busted down to a patrol-car beat on the outskirts of your county. Do you hear me?"

He sat back down, perhaps too quickly, since he winced.

"Hmm. You see, there's a wrinkle in that," Clayton said. "The fact is that Al here isn't even on active duty. He's retired."

"Do you mean to tell me that a private citizen—?"

"Kind of an ad hoc private detective," Al said, not helping things along at all. Regular cops, and especially FBI agents, have an inherent and chronic loathing of PIs. Then he turned to Clayton. "He never said anything at the time."

"You understand the concept of being undercover, don't you?" The agent rose halfway again.

"He does, Aaron," Clayton said. "He's even been undercover."

"You can understand the confusion," Al said. "You came at me. You're lucky I didn't shoot you."

"There's that," Clayton said. "Something to be thankful for. Al often shoots first and asks his questions later."

"Is this funny to you two?" Aaron spun to face Clayton. "You mean this guy's not going to be disciplined, that he's not even any kind of cop? He made one call, and deputies were swarming all over that room."

"He used to be. One of the best detectives I ever had in the department. But, don't you know, he got it into his head that he was aging, getting on, and he up and retired. Yet here I am, plodding on at an age far more advanced than his."

"Where's that red-headed string bean who was with you?" Aaron was shouting as he glared at Al.

"She's following up on the part about why we were there."

"Do you mind telling me what your ex-hotshot was doing crashing a motel photo shoot?"

Clayton suppressed a grin. He turned to Al. "You're on."

"I was looking for a fifteen-year-old girl named Gerta."

"But you didn't find her, did you?"

"No. Turns out Gerta chickened out on the golden opportunity to be in child porn, which you were a conspiring part of, and let her fifteen-year-old classmate Eliska borrow the family car and show up. Now, the last I checked, child porn is still illegal, immoral, and about as low as you can go on my personal crime-watch moral compass."

"Sometimes you have to go along with things to get the big guys at the top." Aaron blushed in spite of himself.

"Well, I've got a missing girl now, who, for all I know, has been kidnapped. Is that the way the Bureau works these days?"

"You know better than that. Kidnapping is still a high priority. I was deeply embedded in something that was taking us a different direction. I have no way of knowing what happened to the girl you're seeking."

"How is it we know nothing at all about your agenda?" Clayton tilted his head as he asked.

Aaron looked away.

"Oh, it's like that, is it? You think someone in the sheriff's department is on the take in this?" Clayton asked.

"We don't know. It just seems we're getting thwarted the closer we get to knowing who's behind this. Someone is tipping them off. We don't know who."

"Mr. Masterson, I've spoken with the Austin agent in charge and his boss, as well—Bryan C. Richards, the special agent in charge of the Houston FBI Field Office. That's the biggest FBI office in Texas. They both think you should have come to me to at least clear this, on the QT if need be. Your immediate superior intends to discuss that with you and suggested you work with someone of my choosing. I should let them surprise you but thought I'd give you a courtesy early heads-up. *Capisce?*"

Aaron nodded, probably already envisioning a pretty peppy conversation with his boss. "But..."

"And since you seem reluctant to work with any of my regular staff, who do you think I'm going to suggest?"

"I don't think so," Al said.

"You haven't got a vote." Clayton looked at Al then panned to Aaron. "And after my talk with your *jefe*, you don't either. So, the two of you, make this happen."

Aaron glanced at Al. "Oh, crap."

"Just don't get in my way," Al said. "I have a mission of my own."

"You're going to go out of your way to get along, Al." Clayton seemed to loom bigger behind his desk as he glared at his former detective. "Or I can make things, let's say... difficult."

Al tilted his head, thought a moment, and turned to Aaron. "Look. I'm sorry we got off on the wrong foot."

"Don't do that."

"What?"

"Refer to your foot."

"Still a little tender in the giblets, eh?"

Aaron gave an eye roll as he turned to Clayton. "Are you sure about this? Old duffer like this is apt to get in my way."

"I think you already know he can handle himself." Clayton chuckled. "And, even retired, he's still the best detective I have."

"Now, how sad is that?" Aaron mumbled.

Chapter Three

Eliska, with a pale round face, horn-rimmed tortoiseshell glasses, and hair like fine yellow corn silk, sat beside a female deputy in uniform across the steel table from Al. He took her in as he eased into his straight-backed metal chair. Its legs squeaked against the hard floor. He hadn't really taken a good look at her in the motel, even though she had been naked. Then she had been wrestling into her clothes before being escorted out of the room by the deputies who arrived on the scene. He'd been keeping a closer eye on the three men in the room.

"Am I being arrested?" She looked at Al then the deputy, Sharah, whose name tag gave her last name as Hansson.

Al knew the deputy only vaguely. She'd been called in for some pat-down searches on female suspects when he'd been active, but like most everyone in the department lately, she seemed barely old enough to be out of high school to Al. He shook his head at the thought, and the girl's eyes opened wider, thinking she had done something to displease him.

"How did you happen to be driving the car belonging to Gerta's mother?"

The girl shrugged and glanced toward the deputy.

"This isn't an interrogation," Al said. "The ones doing something illegal here were those shooting the video and taking the still shots. Whatever happens to you will depend more on your parents."

"My mother's dead. There's just Dad."

"And won't he care?"

She shrugged.

That rubbed Al the wrong way, the same way a teenager saying "whatever" over and over did. He had a flash of thankfulness that he'd never had kids.

However, he saw something in the deputy as well, a flicker in her eyes as she glanced away then back.

Al stood and went to the far corner of the room. The deputy stood as well and came close enough so Al could whisper.

"You know something about the father?" he asked.

"Suspected child abuse is all we've had—wispy suspicions at that. Nothing we could prove, and she wouldn't say. Children's Services was standing by, but we never had enough to make the call."

"I figured there was a reason you were sitting in."

They moved apart and went back to their seats. The girl had turned her head and was looking at herself in the mirror. She patted her hair on one side.

"Do you know where Gerta is?" Al asked her.

Eliska shook her head.

"How did you come to have the car? I need an answer this time."

"It was just there. The keys were in it. So I drove it."

"That would be a felony. Grand theft auto. You may have played the video game."

"Okay, then. She said I could use it."

"Who?"

"Gerta."

The ready lies flowed off the young girl's tongue. She seemed to have had considerable practice.

"You can't have it both ways. Did she tell you to take it, or did you steal the car?"

"She told me to, when she didn't want to go."

"We're going to have to hear her confirming that. I know her mother never said that was okay. Do you have any idea where Gerta is, where she went?"

She shrugged.

"Does she have a boyfriend?"

She shrugged again.

Al started to push his chair back—in anger, he realized. He made himself take a couple of deep breaths. His response and the hard squeak of the chair legs on the floor had snapped Eliska's eyes toward him, as well as the deputy's.

"No shrugs this time," Al snapped. "Do you know?"

"No."

Al heard a knuckle tapping glass. That would be Aaron on the other side of the mirror, which let him watch without being seen and risking his cover being blown.

His agenda was the porn ring, and Al hadn't touched on that yet.

Al sighed. "How did you come to know these men?"

"I didn't. Gerta knew them. When she... when she wanted to back out, I said I'd go. The money. You know."

"How much?"

"The guy said he'd give me a hundred just to see me naked, maybe snap a few photos."

"And to make a video?"

"Five hundred. Maybe even a thousand... if I was real good. I wanted to be real good, do anything. I needed the money."

Chump change. It probably seemed a lot of money to her, though.

"What for?"

"To blow this Popsicle stand."

"And leave your father?"

"Without a look back."

Al couldn't think of anything else to ask. He nodded to the female deputy, who stood.

When Eliska rose to leave the room, Al caught himself taking such a deep breath of air that it sounded like a gasp. The girl wore a white peasant blouse over blue denim short-shorts, so short that three-quarters of her rounded butt cheeks were exposed, as well as a glimpse of what looked like a black lacy thong.

He looked away and caught the deputy suppressing a grin at his discomfort. Eliska was a chubby young thing, probably from a diet of mostly pizzas, burgers, and mac and cheese.

As the deputy escorted Eliska down the hallway, Aaron came out of the room where he'd been looking through the one-way glass. He gave Al a smarmy grin. "What's the matter? Swallow your gum?"

"I think there was a reason I preferred working homicides over this sort of thing," Al said. "We didn't make much progress. What do you have in mind now?"

"The ball's back in my court. Clayton kept the three of us on the porn team separated so the other two wouldn't see me not getting the same treatment they got."

"Which one's the one to worry about?"

"The guy in the bed is just an actor. He's done hundreds of these. He's Kyle Morris, known as Genuine Jim in the porn world. He's six-foot-five and weighs two-fifty. He's probably had more Viagra shoved into him than half the rest of the Travis County male population put together. He gets an HIV test every week and has to carry the paperwork for it to shootings."

"Sounds like quite the life of Riley." Al didn't want to admit that he'd never heard of the guy and wasn't that familiar with the world of porn. However, he bet his brother Maury would know the guy.

"The real player here is the tall one who leaned against the wall. His name's Trick Gibson. He has some priors at this sort of thing, but this is the first time with anyone this young. It would be enough to hold him if that's what we wanted to do."

"But you don't."

"No. We want him running free. I'll hook up with him on the outside, throw a beef about getting hauled in, then see where he takes me. So far, I haven't had a whisper about who the money is behind this."

"He couldn't be doing it all on his own?"

"This is big, Al. There's product getting distributed all through the states and the world. And it's not the kind of thing that flows through regular channels, or it would have been busted long ago. This calls for an ultra-discreet network leading to customers with what we call 'special needs.' Ol' Trick Gibson doesn't have those kinds of chops or connections. I want to find out who does."

"And you'll keep your eye out for Gerta, let me know if you come across her in all this?"

"Sure. Sure thing."

Al doubted that very much. Aaron was an agent with an agenda, and Al was more of a speed bump than a help at that point. He would have to keep on keeping on by himself, or the Bone Lady might just be putting Al's gizzards on display behind the glass at that meat shop.

Chapter Four

Al pulled his truck up in front of his house, turned off the engine, and listened to the motor ticking as it cooled. He had taken to pausing to collect his thoughts before entering his house, which contained a pregnant Bonnie; his brother Maury, who had gotten her that way; and, of course, his rescue dog, Tanner. He kind of wanted to see his dog, but not so much that he wished to brave the emotional roller coaster that was a thirty-six-week-pregnant, still-unmarried Bonnie and a beleaguered Maury. Fergie's car was parked ahead of his truck, so she was inside, too. His home was quite a soap opera for a person who'd thought he was going to live out his retirement years all alone.

As he sat there, a doe came out of the woods to his right. She must have heard him and recognized the truck. She seemed to turn her head and give an "okay" signal to something behind her. Out wobbled a fawn whose spots were so pronounced against his dark back that he couldn't have been very old.

He rushed to his mother's side then shot around her in a burst of energy. Next, the fawn hopped on all fours—boing, boing, boing—then stopped to dash in another direction, only to hop back toward the doe.

The front door opened, and the fawn took off, a bolt of darting speckled brown, while the doe eased off into the woods behind him.

Fergie closed the door, came over to the truck, opened the passenger door, and slid in beside him. "They seem to tolerate you, come to you, but not to the rest of us. They even avoid Tanner, who couldn't care less about them or squirrels and rabbits."

"I fed them through the drought," Al said. "Or it could just be my charming personality."

Fergie shoved his shoulder.

"Did you find anything out about Gerta?" he asked.

"Not much. A boyfriend, maybe," she said.

"For the Bone Lady or Gerta?"

"Gerta."

"And older than Gerta too, I'll bet." Al shook his head. "Who?"

"A promising young loser named E. Z. Ardisson. That's all the Bone Lady knew. That after a long grueling session that included another visit by me, to her home this time. I don't mind telling you that's she's flat-out the scariest woman I've ever been around. And I've seen some pretty hard cases." Fergie shuddered a little. "Whoever might be messing around with her daughter, I hope we get to him before she does... for his sake."

Al might have chuckled had they been discussing anyone else. "The Bone Lady," he said, nearly a whisper.

Fergie shook her head. "Isn't there anything else we can call her?"

"Not and stay on her good side."

"I gotta tell you, Al. She gives me the heebie-jeebies."

"She scares you?" Al shook his head. "Big ol' tough you?"

"Damned straight. Think of it this way. You know I can be tough, but you've also been granted some rather exclusive opportunities to become aware that I can also be soft, very soft, at the right moments. But this woman? Never. She's flint and steel, dawn to dark."

When he didn't respond, she said, "And don't give me a lot of grief on this. I just saw you grinning and looking all moony-eyed at a fawn hopping around the front of your house like it had four pogo sticks for legs."

"How's that...?"

"Admit it. You've come to care about people these days, even animals. That makes you vulnerable too, as long as anything near you can be hurt."

He shrugged. "Old age. It'll do that to you."

"You never used to admit that. Maybe sleeping with someone your own age has changed you."

"Speaking of which..."

She shoved his shoulder again. "I've got the guy's address, this Ardisson. Why don't we drop in and have a chat with him?"

"Sounds good to me." Al reached for the key.

At the same time, Maury came running out the front door. Al rolled down the truck's windows.

"You guys!" Maury shouted. "You've got to help. Bonnie's been bitten by a snake, a copperhead!"

Chapter Five

Al rushed inside, with Fergie and Maury close behind him. He found the usual chaos that had descended on his once-peaceful home had ratcheted up a level.

Bonnie was lying on the floor with a foot up on the coffee table. She was holding her cell phone to her ear.

Tanner ran around and around in circles, not clear on what he could do to help though he clearly knew something was the matter. He rushed to Al as soon as he spotted him. Al rubbed Tanner's head and even gave a speedy rub to the spots behind his ears.

"Lower that foot!" he shouted at Bonnie.

She should have known better—she was a nurse—but it gave him a glimmer of just how rattled she was.

She eased it down at once, tears streaking her rounded cheeks. "The nine-one-one operator doesn't know what I should do."

"Get her to her feet." Al hurried to the fridge and came back holding a bag of frozen peas.

Maury and Fergie stood on either side of Bonnie, holding her upright.

"Let's go." Al tossed the frozen peas to Maury.

They climbed into Fergie's car so that they'd all have room. Maury and Bonnie got into the back seat.

Al peeled out, throwing a spray of gravel toward his truck.

In minutes, they were barreling along, weaving through the country roads. Fergie turned in her seat to keep an eye on Bonnie.

A glance in the rearview mirror let Al see Bonnie's flushed face, covered in a light film of sweat.

"The baby. The baby," she kept saying. Because she was thirty-six weeks pregnant and showing it, the focus of her concern was no surprise.

Al barely braked for curves and pushed the accelerator nearly to the floor. The nearest hospital with an ER was twenty minutes away, forty if rush-hour traffic did its bit. Al flipped on the car's flashers, but not a single car ahead of him pulled over or got out of the way, which was maddening.

"What should we do, Al? What should we do?" Maury pressed the package of frozen peas against the side of Bonnie's foot where they'd all seen the two holes.

"We're doing all we can. We just need to get her professional help. People get snake bit often enough in Texas that someone ought to know what to do once we get there."

"I wasn't an ER nurse, so I never had any training in dealing with a snake bite firsthand, much less being the one bitten," Bonnie said.

"Don't you have a siren in this thing?"

"It's my personal car, Maury," Fergie said. "So no."

"Why don't we talk about something else?" Al suggested.

"All I can think of is little Icky," Maury said.

"We're not naming him that." Bonnie glanced toward Al then fixed on Fergie, who was turned in her seat. "This blockhead wants to name our kid either Ignatz or Ichabod."

"You know it's going to be a boy?" Fergie asked.

"Yeah. We had an ultrasound at twenty weeks. We didn't want to say anything at first. But I guess Maury has decided to reveal that in a public airing."

"The embryo not only had a penis, but it had an erection," Maury said, more than a little pride in his voice.

"The doctor said that sometimes happens." Bonnie glanced over at Maury. "I wasn't altogether surprised."

Al was just glad they kept themselves busy chattering away until he pulled up to the ER. A nurse came hustling out with a wheelchair since they had called ahead.

Bonnie went into another level of hysterics when the check-in nurse said she didn't know what the exact procedure was for a snake-bit pregnant woman.

"You don't know either, and you're a former nurse," she snapped back at Bonnie.

She called for an OB/GYN while a male nurse took what looked like a magic marker and marked a red line that had started up Bonnie's leg.

Fergie stayed close, keeping an arm on Bonnie's shoulder. Al drew Maury away to try to calm him. Maury's eyes were darting left and right, and his breathing was coming in gasps. Al didn't figure Maury could help Bonnie much if he was having his own panic attack.

"Ignatz? Ichabod? What were you thinking? What kind of names are those for a boy?" Al asked.

Maury lowered himself into a chair and looked up at Al. "You know how a kid will ask for an elephant because what he really wants is a pet dog?"

"Not exactly."

"Well, I'm asking for those names so I can push later for what I really want."

"And what's that?" Al was just glad Maury was breathing more easily and seemed to have calmed down.

Two attendants loaded Bonnie onto a gurney. Maury surged to his feet and rushed to her side to hold her hand while they whisked her down the hall. They let Maury tag along and even waved for Al and Fergie to follow, as well, which told Al the situation was not good, not good at all.

"But will antivenom kill the baby?" Bonnie was practically shouting.

"We don't know. We don't know," one of the attendants was saying—not the kind of answer that might calm a nearly hysterical patient.

Just when the chaos was approaching a dangerous level, panic spreading across Bonnie's and Maury's faces, in stepped the doctor—Dr. Laurence Spivey, according to his name plate. He was lean, with almost Einstein-thick grey hair on his head and his mustache almost as white as his coat. Pens sat in the pocket of the lab coat, and one end of a stethoscope was tucked in there, leading up to the headset, hanging loose around his neck. He looked very stern and quite doctorly to Al.

His presence alone had a calming effect on both Bonnie and Maury.

"I'm willing to go a couple of ways here," he said. "But I need you both to know the risks."

That relit some of the panic in their faces, but his soothing, confident tone made a huge difference.

"If you give her the antivenom now, could we lose the baby?" Maury asked.

"It's possible, even likely."

"But what about Bonnie?"

"She's at risk every moment we hold off. She could lose a leg, even die."

"Have you ever done anything like this before?"

"No."

"Will the baby be okay if delivered this early?"

"There's no absolute guarantee of that. He could need help with his breathing. But babies have been born this early before and have turned out fine."

"There's no risk of brain damage?" Maury asked.

"Of course there's a risk. Now, you two have to decide, and quickly. I'll do what I can in either case."

Al started to say something, but Fergie reached and put a hand on his forearm. She was right. The decision belonged to Maury and Bonnie. The call was theirs and only theirs.

Maury glanced toward Al, who nodded at Bonnie.

"What do you think, sweetie?" Maury asked.

Al could have lived out his remaining years without hearing his brother call anyone sweetie, but he could do little about that.

Bonnie's eyes were locked with Maury's. She didn't hesitate. "We save the baby first, if we can, and then worry about me." She turned back to the doctor.

"I'll do everything I can," he said. "As long as you two are aware of everything at stake here. Are you?"

They both nodded.

"Then let's do this thing." The doctor nodded to the nurses, who shooed Al and Fergie out of the room and all the way down the hall to the waiting room.

When the doors closed behind them, Al and Fergie plopped down into a couple of the red Naugahyde chairs with metal arms in the far corner of the room.

"We need to get over to E. Z. Ardisson's place to see if Gerta's there," Al said.

Fergie reached to take his hand. "We need to find out what happens here first."

Al nodded. "You're right." He relaxed into his chair, glanced at the clock, and prepared for a long wait.

Chapter Six

A nurse ushered Al and Fergie into the hospital room. Bonnie looked a little haggard but as happy as Al had ever seen her. She lay on the bed, holding one of the smallest babies Al had ever seen across her chest. The lower part of her snake-bit leg lay outside the sheets, the foot wrapped in gauze. Al thought it looked far less swollen and pink.

She grinned up at them. "We thought he was going to be so small he'd need to be on a breathing machine. But the doctor says he is unusually well developed for his term."

"And well hung." Maury beamed at them. "I might add."

Bonnie cleared her throat. "And we've decided to name him Allard, after a certain someone who stands among us."

"I... I wanted to name him after you all along," Maury said.

Al couldn't argue with that. He felt himself swell a bit inside.

Bonnie bent her head and gave the baby a kiss on the forehead. "All that Ignatz stuff was just a ruse to get his way all along. But I'd have been happy with Al from the get-go."

"You've done so much for us, me especially," Maury said, no doubt sweeping into that statement Al's finally forgiving him for what had kept them from speaking for twenty years: the business with Al's wife, Abbie, the reason Al had never married again.

"How's your leg?" Fergie asked.

"I'll get to keep it. But I won't be dancing the fandango for a week or so." A cloud crossed her face. "But wait until you hear about how much antivenom costs."

"Deciding to go ahead with the C-section was a tough call," Maury said. "We didn't hesitate about the antivenom, even though the doctor explained how much it costs."

"But look." Bonnie reached to pull the sheet aside enough to show more of her bandaged leg. The magic-marker line went all the way to her knee, though the rosy streak from the venom climbing her leg was fading. "At least once we got Little Al safely out of the way, the antivenom could do its thing and save me."

"I... I don't know how we're going to pay for all this." Maury waved vaguely at the hospital around them. "Bonnie's insurance will pay for part of it, but I've got to tell you, Al..."

"Don't forget, we have a wedding to plan and pay for too," Bonnie said.

"I'd heard that antivenom costs a small fortune," Fergie said, "but I have no idea." She glanced toward Al, who had a reputation for knowing trivia.

"A single dose can cost between fourteen thousand and twenty thousand," he said.

"Yikes," Fergie said. "Why so much?"

"The sad part is that the same dose is about a hundred and forty dollars if you happen to be in Canada or Mexico, even less in India."

"What the hell?" Maury said.

"Some blame it on the tangled web that is the lovey-dovey wrestling between big pharma and insurance, with health care right in the middle, getting its share of the pie."

"Some pie. How are we going to pay for this?" Maury said. "I'm in my sixties and haven't worked in a few years."

"We'll work it all out somehow," Al said.

"Yeah, maybe you can sell blood and sperm," Fergie said.

"That's gonna take a lot of sperm." Maury's eyebrows rose.

"You can do it." Bonnie failed to hold back a chuckle.

"Just think, Al. Maury is going to be the star on Father's Day," Fergie said. "He may have had his days of dalliance, but he's surpassed you in one thing."

"You think you and I should get busy and try for a child?" Al asked her.

"Not with me, you won't."

"Why not?"

"Oh, don't talk crazy talk. You know I'm your age, not twenty-five years younger like Bonnie is, which means I'm way past that. Though there's no harm in trying."

Al took in Maury, bending close over Bonnie and reaching in to touch their child. He gave Fergie's arm a tug. "Let's get out of here and leave them to their moment."

They slipped away to the door and were out before either of the new parents looked up.

?

The knock on the door was persistent, relentless.

By the time he had pushed himself up from the ratty-looking couch, after deciding to answer the knocking, he was in a fury.

He swung the door open wide. "What do you want?"

The flash of silver was as quick as a snake's strike.

He looked down and couldn't believe what he saw. A blade was buried all the way to the hilt in his stomach. Then the knife twisted. He felt warm, wet, then hot inside. His vision blurred.

"Why you..." He reached out, not realizing he was already falling backward.

Everything he knew in this world was fading and had gone black by the time he fell to the hardwood floor, twisting the throw rug beneath him.

Chapter Seven

"**I**'d like to take something I said back." Fergie sat in the passenger seat of her car while Al drove.

"What's that?" Al kept his eyes on the road. He was going as fast as he dared to keep from getting pulled over for speeding.

"Earlier, you told the Bone Lady that you had three other cases. I kind of laughed that off if you meant we three who live at your home. But I can see that the Maury-and-Bonnie situation is growing into quite a handful. It was even before the snake bite and birth of a baby. Throw in an impending wedding and a giant hospital bill, and you have a real chunk of hard living rolling at you. Zow!"

"Thanks. Before you brought it up, I was starting to fret a little. Why don't we stay focused here on getting to E. Z. Ardisson's place to see if we can find Gerta?"

He went around a curve a little too quickly and had to brake then accelerate again.

"You wreck my car, you're buying me a new one," she said, a bit of glee at the thrill of the chase showing through. She looked out her side window so he couldn't see her suppressing a smile.

Al had a flickering thought about being back at his once-tranquil home with a crowd of people, a crying baby, and a pile of bills facing him. He shook off that image and fixed on the weaving road ahead.

"We should have been out here hours ago," he said. "If something's happened to Gerta..."

"Blame it on the snake if you need to. It showed little respect for what you had scheduled."

Al turned right at what had once been an old fishing camp of small cabins, too dilapidated to be of any use. He headed down the lane between rows of them toward the lake. He took in the collapsed roofs and yellow paint so chipped that the shacks were hardly painted at all.

He eventually slowed and turned onto the gravel in front of a rustic blue cottage that was not in much better shape than the cabins. The place did at least have a roof and a door, though the door stood half-open.

"Uh oh." Fergie had her hand on the door handle and popped her door open the second Al eased the car to a stop.

He would have paused long enough to get the Sig Sauer out of the glove box had they been in his truck, but they weren't. A Glock was in her glove box, but she left it there, which meant she probably had her ankle holster on under her jeans. He got out, ran toward the gaping door, and went inside right behind Fergie.

"Better not touch anything," she muttered.

He eased closer to look around where she was standing. Al didn't know what E. Z. Ardisson looked like, but he suspected that was him on the floor in a tangled mess of his own blood and part of a throw rug.

"Knife's still here." Fergie pointed.

"Yeah." Al followed her extended finger. "It would be a boning knife. Had to be that, didn't it? Do you see any sign of Gerta?"

Fergie eased around the room's gory centerpiece, hugging the wall as she went around to peek into the lone bedroom and then the bathroom. She came back shaking her head. "There are signs a girl's been here, stuff in the bathroom, but the stiff is the only resident at the moment."

Al reached for his cell phone, hoping his go-to guy among the sheriff's department detectives, Victor Kahlon, wasn't in the middle of anything just then.

Before he had the number all the way punched in, he heard the pounding sound of several men running toward them.

"Boy, this day just gets better and better," Fergie said.

FBI Special Agent Aaron Masterson was the first one through the door, still dressed as Al had last seen him. The lack of sleep showed on his face, as well as a red blush of elevated stress. The two men behind him wore the sort of dark suits Al was used to seeing on Bureau agents.

"You didn't touch anything, did you?" Aaron asked. The men with him rushed to bend over the corpse.

"Of course not," Al said. "I thought you were undercover."

"Not anymore. My cover's blown, and Trick Gibson is as dead as this guy. He got himself blown away."

"And you look good for it?" Al said.

"Perhaps to whoever he reported to, the guy we were after. You haven't forgotten, have you, that he's the one thing I wanted out of all this?"

"Was it knife work?"

"No. It looked like a pro job. Someone held him down and sent a twenty-two shell into each eye. *Ping. Ping.* Close enough to leave powder burns."

"And how about the part you haven't mentioned yet, that Trick and E. Z. are connected somehow?"

Aaron didn't say anything.

"That's what led you here, isn't it? You found something, and now you're here."

"We think so." The words came out reluctantly, but Aaron had promised to work together, no matter how that went against his grain.

"Well, I still have a girl to find. Right now, she looks to be in the middle of whatever mess you're poking at. She was supposed to be here."

"She's connected too, at least in my mind. You probably need to step aside and let us handle finding her now."

"I don't think so. For one thing, the Bone Lady isn't going to want anything to do with anyone who's a fed."

"Who's the Bone Lady?"

"Gerta's mom, who Fergie and I are off to see in a cloud of dust if you don't need us here."

"Go on. Get out of here. But I know where to find you, and I will have to speak with the girl's mother as soon as I wrap up here."

"Well, good luck with that. You're apt to get as much out of her as you will a cigar-store Indian."

Aaron shook his head. "We'll see about that."

Chapter Eight

Al turned off the engine and glanced toward Fergie, in the passenger seat of his truck. "You don't have to come in if you don't want to."

"Yes, I do, or I'll never be able to look at myself in the mirror again."

"That would be a shame. There's a lot of good to see."

"While I appreciate the attempt at flattery, that doesn't stop the butterflies in my stomach from punching each other while doing their clumsy cartwheels."

Al grinned as he walked up the flagstone sidewalk that made a sweep through the green and yellow of an imperfectly grown lawn before stopping in front of a small yellow house with dark-brown shutters. None of it reflected the sort of person who lived within.

He rang the bell, and moments later, the door swung open. The Bone Lady looked out at them. She wore snug jeans and a white blouse tied in a knot at the bottom. She had fastened a red bandana over her head. Al thought she little resembled the woman they'd first seen with a dripping knife in her hand, though he caught a sideways glance of Fergie repressing a shudder.

"Come in," she said. "I was just cleaning."

"Expecting company?" Al asked as he followed her inside.

"Oh, the usual swarm of feds about any minute. I thought you guys might be them now."

A vacuum cleaner stood upright in the center of the living-room rug. Al stepped over the cord.

"You've already heard about what happened to E. Z. Ardisson?" Fergie lowered herself onto one end of the couch.

"Yes. I heard."

34

"The beating of the tribal drums?" Al asked. He eased down beside Fergie.

"Something like that." Some might have grinned at that. She didn't. She remained standing in front of them, arms folded across her chest.

"Do you have any idea who might have done that?" Fergie asked.

"And where Gerta might be now?" Al stayed on mission.

"I didn't do it, if that's your first hunch. Nor do I know who did, or I wouldn't be here waiting."

"When it comes time to do anything about this, I hope you'll leave it to the law or us."

"I trust you more than the feds. But if I hear first..." She let that hang.

Al glanced toward Fergie then back at the Bone Lady. "Gerta hasn't called you, has she?"

"No."

"Do you know a guy named Trick Gibson?"

She shook her head. "Who's he?"

"He shoots porn films. He's the one who tried to lure Gerta. Maybe with a nudge of help from Ardisson."

She nodded slowly, soaking that in. A bit of color showed on her high cheekbones, not anger but a determined will to do something, probably something harsh.

"Trick Gibson is already dead. Someone took care of him, and possibly the same person did E. Z. Ardisson next."

"Gibson was shot," Fergie said. "Gang style with two .22 rounds to the eyes. *Ping. Ping.*"

"With Ardisson, it was a knife, a boning knife," Al said.

"Like I said, it wasn't me."

"You have an alibi?" Fergie asked.

"I was here, by myself, waiting and hoping to hear from Gerta."

"Hmm." Fergie shook her head.

"And you didn't see anything?" Al asked the Bone Lady.

"What do you mean *see*?" Fergie turned to look at him.

Al nodded toward their host. "Maybe you should tell her why they call you the Bone Lady."

She shook her head.

"A long time ago, her people thought she had the gift," Al said. "She could roll the bones and see the future."

"I don't do this for a long, long time," she said.

"But I'll bet you did lately, eh? What did you see?"

She looked away. Then her eyes swung slowly back to them, looking just a little haunted.

"Nothing good," she said. "I saw nothing good at all. In fact, I saw something very, very bad."

Chapter Nine

Al and Fergie entered the hospital room. Maury had roosted at the side of the bed. Bonnie was sitting up with the sheet pulled over what Al guessed was Little Al getting some breakfast.

Maury grinned like the proud papa he was. "How are you guys coming with whatever you're working on?"

"Aside from two people winding up dead so far while we were looking for Gerta," Fergie said, "not so bad. We still have to follow up on a young girl named Eliska, Gerta's friend."

"On that subject," Al said, "do you know a fellow named Kyle Morris?"

"Of course I do," Maury said. "You mean Genuine Jim, right?"

"Maybe you'd better have this conversation in the waiting room or cafeteria," Bonnie said. She seemed to know Morris must be some sort of a porn star if Maury knew the name so quickly. His past was a can of historic worms she didn't seem to wish to open just then.

On their way down the hallway, Maury turned to Al. "You know, I got to see her breast-feeding little Al. Ravenous little fellow, if you ask me."

"Must have been a touching scene."

"Here's the thing, Al. Should seeing that have turned me on? I mean, it really did. I could have pole-vaulted out of the room."

"I suspect a cricket crossing its legs might turn you on, Maury."

They took their cups of coffee over to a table in the corner of the cafeteria, near a row of windows that confirmed that the day was going to be bright and shining. As soon as they had settled in their seats, Fergie took a sip of her coffee and shuddered.

"Pretty bad?"

37

"Well, if you like the slight taste of burnt oil from a big commercial urn that hasn't been cleaned nearly as often as it should, then you'll be fine. Drink up!"

"Anyway"—Al turned back to Maury—"is this Morris guy the sort you could envision in something like child porn?"

Maury started to chuckle but, seeing their expressions, shifted to coughing and clearing his throat. "Fact is, I could picture him in about anything. He's been in every kind of situation you can imagine. Straight. Gay. Even some tranny stuff." A touch of admiration showed in Maury's voice, which Al could have done without.

"This isn't Hollywood, and he's not up for an Oscar." Fergie's scowl was no longer about the coffee. "Have you ever seen him in any kind of child porn?"

"Of course not. That stuff is as gone from the Internet as a dodo's left testicle. You post or download or even view something like that, and the feds would swoop in on you, and that would be that. Even the subtle swapping between the twisted aficionados in that field has led to raids and arrests. I've got to say I'm okay with that. Child porn is as hard for me to understand as a foot fetish. Now, you take a ripe, middle-aged plum like Bonnie, and—"

"Stick with us here, Maury," Al said. "If they can't make their money from these films through the regular, so-called legit channels, how do they market the stuff? There must be money in it, or they wouldn't do it in the face of such heat."

"There are probably small groups of like-minded persons who keep in touch somehow. They probably have a common bond based on age—not their own ages, the ages of the type of kids they prefer. Some may like the almost-legal ones, like you're dealing with. Others follow the kink ladder all the way down to infants."

"It is so handy, Al, that your brother knows so much about an area where the perps just ought to be strung up."

"Hey, don't kill the messenger. I'm just giving you guys a tiny bit of background on what you asked about."

"That's right." Al looked in Fergie's direction. "What else? How would they connect?"

Maury hesitated. After a quick glance at Fergie, he said, "Given the current heat on such things"—his eyes flicked toward her again—"and deserving heat it is, they probably have to be very careful about using anything electronic to connect. You can bet the feds have that thoroughly covered and have already caught enough folks in the space to make the others extremely wary. Maybe small pods of them meet in person at giving places, use a code of some sort in ads to know where to meet. They certainly can't lean on Kik groups."

"What are Kik groups?" Fergie asked.

"They're public and private groups you can join to meet others. Kik groups are chat rooms you can reach through a smartphone messenger app that lets you exchange text messages, even photos. You can even search to see if there are any dirty groups you can join. But someone has to let you in. And they can kick you out for the least little thing. You can just bet the FBI has people assigned to keeping track of as many of those as possible that might dance close to their target areas."

"I think we can count on the feds for following up on a lot of the possible public or semipublic ways to connect," Al said. "What do you think is our best bet for tracking any of these distinguished citizens?"

Maury shook his head. "You'd almost have to find a person you know who is in on some of this and track backwards from there. See how that person reaches out. But I have to warn you that there may be many, many ways. Off-the-grid ways. Ones even the highly sophisticated trackers for the various federal, state, and local law enforcement agencies have failed to discover."

"You make it sound so easy," Fergie said.

"Oh, it's anything but easy," Maury said. "This may well be some of the toughest detecting you've ever come across in both of your lives."

Chapter Ten

"It's very hard to know where to start, isn't it?" Fergie glanced at Al.

He was sitting in the passenger seat because she had wanted to drive her own car back to the house. He'd been mulling over any number of useless possibilities and didn't mind the break from driving.

Some cases were like a Gordian knot—complex, but at least he could see the knot. In this case, Al could see nothing. Anything like a lead had petered out. He could thrash around, but until he had a thread of something, that would just be wasted effort, as much as it would feel good to be doing something, anything.

The usual scenery of the few houses and wide patches of green woods rolled by as they got closer to his home.

He sat up straighter. "Pull over up ahead, would you?"

He could hear the rasp of a chainsaw chewing away at the trunk of a thick mountain cedar as they passed the property next to his. Fergie pulled over at the edge of a buffer lot he'd bought against the prospect of anyone building too close to his house as the urban sprawl of Austin marched out toward his edge of the lake.

Media reports indicated Austin was growing at the rate of something like 220 people per day, and they were all bringing vehicles. None of the roads had grown quickly enough to keep up. Even out as far as his place was from the city, he could hear chainsaws and chippers in several directions. Above that came hammering and the sound of nail guns as the structures of houses went up and roofs were pounded into place.

A spot of red flashed back in the thickness of green, the chainsaw whined, then another mountain cedar fell over to join several already sprawled on their sides. Ahead lay his house. Soon, his place would be much more exposed to the road and those passing on it.

"All this together is really stressing you out, Al." Fergie paused. "I mean a difficult case, Bonnie's baby, and the coming bills. You know. All that. And now this on top of everything."

"What makes you say that?"

"You should see the vein in your neck. It's just throbbing away like Gene Krupa showing off on his drum set."

"That kind of thing dates us, knowing who Gene Krupa was."

"We're in our sixties. We both know what age we are though one of us is slower to admit it. Get over it."

The guy cutting out the cedar saw the car and turned off the chainsaw. He headed their way. The usual process with such properties was to clear out the mountain cedar, chip it into mulch or just have it hauled away, and leave only the live oaks standing alone to lend shade to the house and yards. Al hadn't expected to see that happen in his lifetime. *Maybe I'm just living too damned long*, he thought.

He felt the way he did when he parked way out in a parking lot at a mall store or grocery, all alone, and then some yahoo swung in and parked right next to him, with Al thinking, "Are you just lonely, or what?"

"Can I help you folks?" The guy looked about the same age as Al but wore blue jeans and a long-sleeved red sweatshirt on what was turning into a 107-degree-heat-index day. The shirt was soaked through in a wide wet vertical stripe, front and back. His worn ball cap was black with a burnt-orange longhorn-steer logo for the University of Texas on the front.

As soon as Al climbed out of the car, the guy said, "Oh. You must be Al Quinn."

"I don't know if I must, but I am." Al reached for the hand the man held out after tugging off a glove.

"I'm Harley Struthers, and you are, of course, Al Quinn."

"This is Fergie. Formerly Detective Ferguson Jergens."

"You're a cop too? Good."

"We're both pretty retired," Fergie said, "when we can be."

"I was told that living this close to you, Al, would mean I'd pretty much get left alone out here."

"I don't know who told you that, but I wish they'd told me the same thing."

The guy glanced around at the fallen cedars and one pile of brush he'd begun to accumulate. "I've owned this property for years and years. I would come out and visit it now and then but wasn't sure if I'd ever do anything with it."

Al thought to himself that he'd been hoping it would be left alone as well.

"The wife and I are retired, had hoped to just while away our days in an apartment. But the prices of rent and everything else in town just kept on climbing, and I had this land, so here I am. It's a nice piece of property."

"Yeah, a whole lot of fawns were born on it."

"And I hope the deer will feel welcome to have more here when I and the missus are all settled. That shouldn't be long. I have a son and son-in-law who plan to come out and help clear the land, keeping the live oaks, of course. Once I see what I've got after that, I can lay out plans. Pouring the slab and building the house and garage should start in November."

"That's wise. Building when it's cool." Al looked around. He could already see most of his house from there. *Ah, well.* He'd like to have stoked his anger, being upset at life crowding in on him once more, but the guy was just too darned nice for that.

He and Fergie shook Harley's hand one more time and headed for her car. She didn't look at him right away, seeming to understand he needed a moment or two to come to peace with himself.

Al slid into the passenger seat and looked through the spare trees of his buffer lot on the closer side. He could see most of his house and a stretch of the hill out back, leading down to the lake and his boat dock and fishing dock. He blinked. A boat was just pulling up to his dock, and a man leaped out of it to scurry across it to head up the hill toward the house.

"What fresh hell is this?" He turned to Fergie.

"Did I just see...?"

"Let's roll. Pronto."

Chapter Eleven

Fergie turned the engine off early and let her car roll to a stop in front of the house.

Al used the time to get her Glock out of the glove box. He jacked a shell into the chamber and was out the door and running alongside the house as soon as the car stopped.

He came around the corner just as the guy was prying at the back door with a long-handled crowbar. Tanner was barking and growling inside. The door popped open, and the guy started inside.

Al was running flat out.

The guy burst inside. The growling and barking from Tanner grew to a maddening crescendo.

Still going full speed, puffing like some antique steam engine, Al ran along the back of the house and rushed inside the doorway just as the guy swung a leg back to kick at Tanner.

Al reached low with his left hand, grabbed the ankle, and jerked straight upward.

The guy rose and flipped forward, and his head smashed face-first onto the hard basement floor.

Without a second's hesitation, Al flipped the man over onto his back and brought his right hand, holding the gun, down on the man's face hard as he could, three times. *Pow. Pow. Pow.* Then he stopped, breathing hard. The guy lay there, eyes closed and out of it.

Panting, Al stepped across the guy to reach out his arms, and Tanner shot into them and licked him on the face.

"Oh my heavens." Fergie stood behind him just outside the open door. "Who is that?"

"I guess we'll find out soon enough."

Al stood, and they carried the guy out to an ash tree, put his arms around it, and used his own handcuffs to fasten him to the trunk. Fergie tossed the man's gun aside and held up the black leather credentials case. "Surprise!"

Al walked over to the top of the hill and looked down. Whoever was waiting in the boat spun it and revved the motor as he raced away from the dock, going so fast he nearly threw a rooster's tail.

"So much for a faithful sidekick," Al muttered.

He glanced over at the fallen man, slumped with his face against the tree, still out for the count. Tanner came out and peed on the guy's leg. Al shrugged but chuckled a little in spite of himself.

He dug out his wallet and took out the card Aaron had given him. He punched in the number.

Aaron answered almost at once.

"I've got something of yours," Al said. "Or should I say someone."

"You listen to me..."

Al hung up.

?

Aaron must have had to come all the way out during rush hour from somewhere deep in the city. He got there fifteen minutes after Sheriff Clayton himself arrived at Al's house.

Clayton was sitting in a lawn chair beside Fergie and Al's. All of them were within range of the tree, where the agent had come to and was sharing some language that would have made most people blush had they not all been seasoned law officers.

Aaron came stomping around the side of Al's house, already cussing as much himself. "You have one helluva lot to explain!" He stopped shouting the moment he realized who was sitting in the chair beside Al. "What are you doing here?"

"I thought I told you two to work together, get along," Clayton said. His voice came across as a low rumble.

"I... I..."

"I don't think Al is the one with any explaining to do here. Do you?"

Aaron looked around at each of them, then to the tree. "Let me get Purvis off of there."

"Not just yet," Clayton said. "I think he likes it there."

"No, I don't!" Purvis yelled. One cheekbone had swollen to about the size of a grapefruit, and he was going to have a righteous shiner on that eye for a good while.

"You are interfering with a federal investigation," Aaron tried.

"I don't think so. What we're interfering with is a B and E. This might just explain a rash of them we're having in the county." Clayton was very close to breaking into a chuckle.

"I don't see how you think this is funny." Aaron's face grew a brighter pink.

"I don't." Clayton sat upright. "And neither does Bryan C. Richards, with whom I had the most invigorating discussion not ten minutes ago."

"What... what did he say?"

"I'll let him share his thoughts with you—and believe me, he is eager to do so—once we're wrapped up here."

"Let me get my colleague, and we'll go."

"I don't think so. Get the man a chair, Al."

"What about me?" Purvis yelled.

"Pipe down," Al said. He unfolded a chair and put it down beside Aaron, who settled slowly into it. He had the look of a captain going down slowly with his ship.

"First things first," Al said. "You owe me for a door."

"Put in a chit," Aaron said.

"I don't think so," Clayton rumbled. "Pony up. Then *you* put in a chit."

Aaron grumbled but pulled out his wallet. He counted out three hundred fifty dollars, all in large bills, which he put into Al's extended hand.

Al shook his head and wiggled his fingers.

Aaron looked at Clayton then took out another hundred and put it in Al's hand as well.

Al shrugged and shoved the money into his jeans pocket.

"Now to business," Clayton said. "What in all-fired blazes were you thinking, pulling a stunt like that?"

"I... I don't have a quick answer."

"Give me a slow one, then."

Aaron glanced at Al then at Purvis, who hugged the tree, looking as uncomfortable as Al had ever seen an FBI agent. The scene reminded him a little of Christmas, with decorations on a tree. Had the man not tried to kick Tanner, he might have felt a little sympathy too.

"We were getting nowhere. This is the damnedest mess. Every lead we had was gone. I even had someone take a shot at me. Blew out the windshield of my rental car but missed me, barely."

"And what did you think you might get by breaking into Al's house?"

"Something. Anything. There was the barest chance he had tumbled onto something. So we were going to..." He stopped.

"We found the bugs on Purvis. We know what you were going to do." Clayton glanced toward Al. "Do you know anything that's worth sharing at this point with Aaron?"

"No. I wish I did. But I have about as much as he does," Al said. "Except no one else thinks I know enough to start shooting in my direction."

"I was desperate," Aaron said.

"No excuse. But I'll save that tongue-lashing for your boss and his boss. They are both quite eager to speak with you. Apparently, you've been dodging their calls."

"I thought I might be able to straighten this out among us."

"What you thought is you might be able to bully your way clear, using what you think is your federal clout."

Aaron started to speak but closed his mouth instead.

"Is there any advice you might give Aaron here?" Clayton looked to Al.

"Yeah. About the only single particle of anything active going on in all this is that someone, a Bu someone, thinks he knows enough that he needs to be eliminated the way Trick Gibson and E. Z. Ardisson were. I think he should stake himself out like a goat and hope that bait brings whoever is behind this closer, and then have his men grab that person if they're in time."

Aaron swallowed so loudly Al was sure they all heard it.

Chapter Twelve

"Do you know what you remind me of?" Fergie asked.

"No. What's that?" Al pulled his truck over in front of Armand Grunderson's house. He had driven up a black asphalt lane that made a loop by the front door and headed back the quarter-mile to the two-lane ranch-to-market road.

The house was tucked deep in the woods, the trees surrounding the place on all sides. Split-level and made of a white stone like aged gypsum, it could've been mistaken for something Frank Lloyd Wright had planned and built, a reminder that Grunderson was an architect. A row of yellow and red flowers ran along the base—not the sort of thing Al had been expecting at all. A run-down place would have fit the picture in his head better.

"You're like that bloodhound when it's just been dropped on the ground and doesn't know where to begin, so it starts casting about in wider and wider circles hoping to get a scent of something."

"I can't disagree with that. Only the dog probably possesses more hope of stumbling onto something than I do just now."

Al had barely clicked the brass door knocker a couple of times when the front door swung open.

"Armand Grunderson?" Al asked.

The man nodded. He stood taller than Fergie's six-two and looked as lean and hard as a lifelong ranch hand, instead of an architect who designed the many new houses filling the developments sprawling outward from the core of Austin. His sparse red hair was thinning and combed back above a long, tanned rectangular face that led down to a slightly larger-than-normal chin. He looked as little like his pale, roundish daughter Eliska as possible.

"Yes. What now?" He spoke in a precise, controlled way, which Al figured out in a flash. The man spoke with a stiff upper lip, the way British speakers do.

"May we come in?"

"I suppose. Everyone else has."

"Everyone?" Fergie asked.

"The FBI."

"That's all?"

"It was enough."

The narrow foyer opened to a sprawling living room with a glimpse of a kitchen and dining area off to the right. A wrought-iron spiral staircase climbed upstairs to the left.

Grunderson led them down a short hallway past the staircase to a den that also served as his drafting room and office. He probably felt most comfortable there.

Outside, a koi pond with bright-green lily pads and cement frogs was where most people might have put a swimming pool.

A framed photo was centered above the fireplace mantel. Al eased close enough to see what held the honored spot. Grunderson stood with his arm around Eliska, the red hull of a wooden ship behind them. Whoever had been standing on the other side of Eliska had been cropped out, and the photo had been recentered in raised white matting. Al knew that boat, part of the Red Dragon Pirate Cruises out of Port Aransas. The event was a fun family memory, now only a partial one, given the missing portion of the image, probably Eliska's mother and Grunderson's late wife.

The wife had died in an auto accident that wasn't her fault. Al had made the effort to check the backstory on that—nothing fishy at all there. Like most police reports, the one about the accident gave Al no information that might help, like whether the couple got along, how they treated their daughter, and what kind of tailspin her death had sent Grunderson into. That he'd cut her out of the happy family portrait suggested a couple of possible ways to interpret how their lives together had been.

Al and Fergie settled into matching guest chairs while their host eased into a Herman Miller Eames chair behind an ornate oversized vintage mahogany desk. The effect was like students being called into the school principal's office. Al figured that wasn't by accident.

Grunderson was staring at Fergie.

"What did the FBI want to know?" Al asked.

Grunderson's head swung toward Al. "If you're working with them, then they're the ones you should ask."

"Do you have any idea where Eliska's friend Gerta is?" Fergie asked.

"No." Grunderson seemed eager enough to focus on her again.

"Is Eliska here? And can we speak with her?" Fergie glanced toward the door.

"No."

"She's not in?"

"No."

"Do you know where she is?"

"No."

Al shifted in his chair at the conversation, which was like speaking to someone from Maine, who had eleven words a year to use and had already spent half of them.

"Aren't you worried about her whereabouts?" Fergie asked.

"She's mature for her age and is capable of being on her own from time to time."

"If, for instance, you needed to speak with her right now about something pressing," Al butted in, "do you have any idea where you might look for her?"

Grunderson frowned at him, his lips pressing tighter.

"Please," Fergie said.

"Oh, probably at that damned mall where the lot of them hover around like pretend adults while saying 'awesome' to the point one wishes to vomit."

That at least struck a sympathetic chord with Al, who had recently said pretty much the same thing about the word "whatever."

?

Outside, the growing heat of the day slammed into them until they slid inside the truck and Al jacked the AC up as high as it could go to clear out the heated interior.

"First impressions?" Al asked.

"He could do it. Putting aside his hoity-toity attitude, he's as earthy and primal at core as any man I've ever seen. Even Maury on his most horndog days didn't cast out such an aura eager to climb onto a woman, any woman, and have his way with her."

"I didn't pick up on all of that."

"Men rarely do." She looked out her window as the house faded in the distance behind them. "Where to now?"

"I'd like to look in at the mall. And if time permits, I wouldn't mind having a chat with the star of that motel movie moment, Kyle Morris, or Genuine Jim as he's known in the porn world. If you're feeling a little starstruck, you might ask for his autograph."

"I wouldn't wipe my behind with his autograph."

"Good to know you're not prejudiced."

They had to park a blistering quarter-mile walk out in the parking lot and finally staggered into the cool interior of the mall. The upper and lower levels of stores all sought to have inviting entrances, but the noise of occasional shouts and squeals rose above the hubbub of people out getting yet another pair of shoes or being fitted for glasses at the eyewear store.

Fergie steered them toward the food court, the mixing bowl of America's youth. Al recalled when the local drive-through restaurant, Shively's, was the hot spot in his teens. A friend of his had been on the way to the hospital once after an appendicitis attack but mustered the strength to lift himself up onto his elbow on the gurney to call out to the driver, "Once through Shively's."

As soon as they entered the space and smelled a mixed medley of scents, from cinnamon rolls to pizza, Al knew something was up. Those sitting at the tables and milling about were far too subdued. He needed only seconds to spot the cause. One fellow was leaning against the wall next to a Chinese food vendor and the entrance hallway to the restrooms. He wore a blue long-sleeved jacket over khaki slacks.

Another sat on the far side at a table. Wearing a light tweed jacket, he took an occasional sip from what looked like a seventy-two-ounce paper cup of iced tea.

The woman on the team was harder to spot. Her eyes gave her away, though. They pierced like two spears through the crowd as she fussed over a stroller that Al was pretty sure didn't contain a real baby.

Leave it to the FBI to turn casual into intense. Even the food-court patrons who didn't know exactly what was going on felt the palpable nature of it and spoke in more subdued voices than usual.

"Let's get out of here," Fergie muttered. "Someone's peed in this watering hole."

Chapter Thirteen

"You know, Al," Fergie said, "I suspect in your case that you have always struggled against giving in to lust and being like your brother Maury."

Al glanced her way as they wove through Austin's traffic to the downtown penthouse where Morris lived. He tried to give her a raised eyebrow the way she could, but he wasn't sure he pulled it off.

"I think that since Abbie, you have fended off any feeling of love. You can deal with infatuation and temporary intimacy, but not the vulnerability of commitment and true love."

"What brought that on?"

"I guess wading through the seamy side of male culture makes me rethink the distinction between lust and love."

"You know I care about you."

"Yeah. Yeah. Trust me, after Grunderson and our upcoming meeting with Kyle 'Genuine Jim' Morris, you're going to come out looking like a saint with spurs. So, no need to feel defensive."

"Then why do I?"

They parked in a pay lot half a block away and walked to the apartment building. The sun had grown hot enough to remove eyebrows, which made the icy air of the lobby nearly unpleasantly chill.

The elevator was so quiet they could hear only a dull ping as the door opened onto the top floor.

Fergie rapped on the apartment door.

Al heard muffled steps coming, then the door swung open. Kyle wore dark leather sheepskin-lined slippers and a loose white shin-length robe, underneath which, Al suspected, was little else. His curiosity wasn't such that he cared to know for sure.

Kyle waved them inside with a sigh. "What now?" It came across as, "Why poor me?" The beleaguered star was annoyed in his usually protective cave of solitude.

The front hallway was lined with pictures, stills from films. None of them showed him nude, at least not all the way there. Among them, one exception stood out, a photo of Kyle beside an older version of himself, both wearing hunting jackets, an arm around each other's shoulders. Al wondered if the father knew in what kind of films Kyle starred. He suspected he did and might even be proud of his son.

The interior of the apartment, or suite, sprawled all the way to picture windows that ran floor to ceiling along the far two walls. Al could see the edge of the capital building and the Methodist church, as well as the portion of downtown that stretched out to the south.

A row of exercise equipment—including a treadmill, an elliptical bike, a bench with free weights, and a rowing machine—lined the windows.

"I have to work out at home to keep in shape for my job. I can't go to gyms, or I get swarmed by adoring female fans."

"I didn't know females watched your sort of product," Fergie said.

Kyle ignored her lip curl. "Oh, they do. Some of them do. Quite a bit more than you'd expect."

"I'm surprised to find you at home," Al said. "Aren't there charges against you of one kind or another?"

Kyle shrugged. "I didn't know her age. Couldn't know. Trick Gibson showed me false papers that indicated the girl was eighteen."

"And you couldn't tell by looking at her that there was no way she was anything like eighteen?" Fergie asked.

"No. I couldn't. I doubt if most people can. The producers look for people who look young. That's what a lot of the public wants. Anyway, I can't talk about this much. My lawyer is handling my insignificant little part in this thing."

Al looked around the apartment. Everything looked expensive and top-shelf. Aside from the hardship of having to take a valium about every five minutes, the so-called star was doing well for himself and probably had a pretty good retirement package coming together, as well as a top-gun lawyer under retainer.

"I can't believe you're out on your own and that no charges have been filed," Fergie said.

"Not even on my own recognizance, as my lawyer tells me." Kyle's grin was what Al figured the British would call smarmy. "He explained that the Child Exploitation Enterprise statute alone requires the government to prove quite a bit, including offenses of at least three incidents and more than one underage victim being involved."

"I doubt very much that the Child Exploitation Enterprise statute had anything to do with what could have been the charges against you if there had been enough to hold you." Fergie was starting to speak through her teeth, never a good sign.

To Al, that sounded like so much bovine droppings shoveled on by a lawyer. Since Kyle could claim he was duped and had no priors, that would make it hard for an arrest to hold. With a good story and a good lawyer, Kyle was likely to get off without so much as a finger slap. If he stayed with regular adult porn going forward, he should be okay—legally, if not morally.

Al glanced toward Fergie and decided he'd better do any further talking himself. "We're missing a girl, maybe two girls now. Do you have any idea where they might be?"

"Not the foggiest. I have nothing to do with delivering the talent. I don't even know their names, or I forget them if I do."

"So all this is just a tiny bump of inconvenience in the road to you, isn't it?"

"Not even so much as that," Kyle said. "This bit of notoriety has sent a ripple through the industry, added a bit of sizzle to my name. My agent says his phone is ringing off the hook."

Fergie's face grew stern and flushed in anger at Kyle's smug look. "What I want to know..."

Al reached out a hand and stopped Fergie from where she was headed. They had learned all they were going to. He'd just wanted to see the man again, and they'd done that.

"We'd better get ourselves back to the hospital. Okay?" He eased a reluctant Fergie toward the door.

She didn't speak until they were halfway down in the elevator. "Normally, I'd bust your chops for not letting me say what was on my mind. But in this case, you were probably right. Even now, as I hear the words in my head, they in no way lead to making the planet a kinder and gentler place."

Chapter Fourteen

Maury and Al headed out the hospital room's door.
As soon as they were outside the room, Fergie turned to
Bonnie, who lay in her bed with the covers up to her chin. The baby
could have been off in the nursery, but he was asleep in a small bed in
the room instead since Bonnie was breastfeeding.

"I take it you really didn't want ice cream," Fergie said. "You just
wanted to get the men out of the room for a moment."

"Yeah," Bonnie admitted. "Except I wouldn't mind the ice cream,
either. How's your investigation coming along?"

"Lost in the swamp for the moment. But that might clear up soon...
or not." Fergie glanced over at the baby. She had a hunch about what
might be in Bonnie's craw at the moment. "Are you two planning on
getting married now?"

Bonnie started to chuckle. That turned into a laugh she tried to sti-
fle so that she wouldn't wake the baby, and that made her cough. She
wiped at her eyes with a tissue while Fergie waited.

"You know, I wasn't going to say anything, but Maury and I have
even gotten so far as sampling wedding cakes," Bonnie said.

"So? Lots of people do that."

"We had a kind of fight about it."

"Why?"

"He liked a cake I thought was just plain bitter."

"And?"

"When I asked him why, he said he thought wedding cakes were
supposed to be bitter. 'Symbolism,' he said."

"Oh, my. Maybe he was just joshing."

"He knows better than to josh with me about that."

Fergie didn't know what to say, so she stayed silent.

"Do you think I'm making a mistake marrying someone like... well, like he was?" Bonnie asked.

"He *was* a womanizer. That's for sure. He told Al once that for college he planned to study 'a broad.' But I think you tamed a lot of that out of him."

"Some with a cast-iron skillet."

"All the same, you've been through a lot together. I think he genuinely cares about you. Do you care as much about him?"

"Yeah, I guess I do. But could that just be a reverse Stockholm syndrome or something?"

"Only you can answer that. But I suspect not. And you've already had a child together."

"A darn beautiful one too. I'm glad to have had Little Al. But how are we gonna support him? I'm not letting Al pay me anymore to tend to Maury as a nurse."

"Even though that may have been some sort of atonement on Al's part for not speaking to Maury for twenty years?"

"Maury had that coming for the way he messed up Al's marriage and all. I can always go back to nursing, but what can Maury do? Work as a door greeter at some chain store?"

"Don't get ahead of yourself. Everything might sort itself out on its own."

"Or not. What then?"

Fergie didn't have a quick answer for that.

?

As the three of them headed out to his truck, Al turned to Maury. "Getting away from there for a spell, grabbing a shower and a nap will be good for you. We can bring you back in later as we wind our way through this currently clueless case. How's everything going with you?"

"It's an emotional roller coaster around here most days," Maury said.

"I'm guessing it's even more so for Bonnie since her body is struggling to get back to normal," Fergie said as she climbed into the back seat of Al's extended cab.

"Yeah, I guess so. What about you guys? Have you wrapped up what you were working on?"

"Not very likely." Al started his truck and drove through the lot. He eased up to the stop sign that led out to the street and paused to look both ways. "We haven't even landed on a very good place to start."

"Nothing really big has happened for a short spell," Fergie said.

A crack on the windshield sounded like a big bug hitting the glass as hard as it could. Al glanced that way. A tennis-ball-sized hole had been smashed in through the safety glass.

"What the hell?" Fergie asked.

"I'm hit, Al. I'm hit!" Maury cried out. He held his left hand up to his right shoulder.

Al hit the gas hard and spun the truck to the right so that he would be on the side where the shooting had come from.

"Where are you going?" Fergie bounced around in the back seat.

"Away from whoever's shooting." He took the truck up the street half a block. He pulled over and flipped open the glove box. He took out his Sig Sauer, opened his door, and took off running up the street.

As he ran, he tried to fix every detail he'd seen in his mind. He couldn't recall seeing a vehicle parked across the street. The shot might have come from a thick clump of junipers.

He eased his way up to those, leaped inside, and waved his gun around at nothing. The grass was thick underfoot, so no footprints were there, but he did spot the brass glitter of a shell casing. He used a twig to pick it up and drop it, still warm, into his shirt pocket. He looked around on the other side of the junipers. Anyone on the ground could have run off in any direction, and he saw no indication of which way. Even the bent grass of the lawn didn't show distinct footprints. Besides, he had to get back to Maury.

He jogged back to his truck. No hospital security or anyone else was coming to it. Fergie was holding a cloth pressed hard to Maury's shoulder. His face, though, had washed pale.

"You've got to get me to a hospital, Al," Maury said.

Al climbed behind the wheel and tossed the gun back into the glove box and closed it. "I've got the first bit of really good news for you, Maury, on an otherwise pretty shitty day. We don't have far to go, not very far at all."

He spun the truck around and headed back to the hospital, not stopping until he pulled up in front of the ER doors.

Chapter Fifteen

"**W**hy would someone try to kill me?" Maury sat up on the exam table, the white paper stretched beneath him crackling with every move he made.

An ER doctor was cleaning the wounds, front and back. A nurse beside him held a gauze pad ready.

"A clean through-and-through," the doctor muttered.

"What have I done to anyone?" Maury asked. "Other than knock up Bonnie?"

"I think it's just a not-very-competent shooter," Fergie said.

"Or more than one person. One was quite capable when it came to dealing with Trick Gibson. It might have been a different person who did the knife work on E. Z. Ardisson."

"Not the Bone Lady, I hope," Fergie said.

"We'd be glad to discuss all your theories if you'd just step outside here a moment."

Al looked toward the doorway and saw Sheriff's Department Detective Deputy Victor Kahlon. Beside him stood someone who was probably a city detective Al didn't know.

Fergie did, though. "Well, Moose Tarleton. I'd thought you'd be a doughnut away from retirement by now."

The big-city detective chuckled. His blue gabardine sports coat was rumpled, and the white front of his shirt bulged out the front of it. "Well, you know, Fergie, gunshot wound reported at a hospital. Someone's gotta look into it."

He was the same height as Victor but looked bigger. He was, at the very least, heavier.

"And I'm along for comic relief. Also because part of this case oozes out into the county, and Clayton said I'd better see what Al's turned up this time."

Al fished a latex glove out of a box on the counter and slipped it on to retrieve the shell casing from his pocket.

Since the shooting had happened in the city, Moose took an envelope out of his pocket. Al dropped the casing in after Moose gave it a quick glance.

"Thirty-ought-six," Moose said. "Hardly a squirrel gun, and certainly not something to be shooting within the city limits."

"Not to mention making noise in a hospital zone," Al said.

?

Al sat in the lobby of Longhorn Glass, a business across I-35 from the University of Texas campus. The business had just the small waiting area and a checkout counter. The rest of the building had a row of garages where a waiting line of vehicles got new windshields, side windows, or whatever they needed. The roar of cars on the overpass above rattled the front pane of the store's picture window. Motivational posters and a general encouragement for everyone there to have fun at what they did made the wait easier, along with the fact that he'd have his truck back in twenty minutes or so. Al liked the place. The last time he'd gone there, they'd even moved his registration and inspection stickers to the new windshield.

The front door swung open, and a head leaned in. Al sighed and shook his head. FBI Special Agent Aaron Masterson came all the way inside and headed toward him.

"Detective Ferguson Jergens told me where you'd be."

"Where's your entourage?"

"Out in the car, waiting." Aaron glanced out the front window. "I hope you don't mind me dropping by."

"Of course I mind."

"We're supposed to be working together, cooperating."

"I'll be up front and frank with you if you want."

"Sure."

"When you start caring as much about this missing girl Gerta as you do your own career, I'll start to believe there's hope for you."

"You think I'm...?"

"Overzealous? You're damned right I do."

"You have to stand up for yourself if you want to get ahead in the Bu. I guess you wouldn't understand since your time was spent..."

"Protecting and serving. Not ignoring the plight of human children by shooting them in porn videos just to go after those higher in that sad food chain."

"It had to be done." Aaron looked away then back at Al, who hadn't risen from his seat. "I guess you don't think much of me."

"You'd be right about that. Maybe there's hope for you yet. This rodeo is far from over."

"I just stopped by since I was shot at and you were shot at. Maybe there was some parallel, something you noticed."

"All that's in a statement I left with Moose and Victor. They have the thirty-ought-six shell casing as well. They're the ones you should be talking to about that."

"I've spoken with them, heard all they had to say."

"Then do some good, solid detection work and quit swashbuckling around. You're not Errol Flynn. You're a member of law enforcement with the appropriate training, just as I once was."

"I am making all the right steps as far as they take me."

"Then you've spent too many hours watching spy films and not enough time opening your heart to truly empathize with those you're supposed to be protecting and supporting."

"And you're good at that?"

"No. I'm hopelessly flawed. But I'm working on it, however badly, and that gives me the bulge on you."

Aaron's indignant chest inflated like a rooster claiming territory. "I'll have you know I make a concerted effort to stay emotionless whenever possible. Detached. It's called professionalism. You should try it."

"Your vehicle's ready, Mister Quinn," the chubby girl grinning behind the counter said.

Al went over and paid and got his key back. He listened to the spiel about not driving over sixty for a day or two, lest the window pop out before it had a chance to set all the way.

He turned around. Aaron was gone. *Good.* Al could have done without Clayton's urging to get along with the feds. He'd done so many times before, with rarely a problem, but that guy was surely the bad pickle in the barrel.

Al went out to his truck and climbed inside. The windshield was clearer than ever. He smiled to himself as he headed back to the hospital to pick up Fergie.

Chapter Sixteen

"The sheriff said I was to cooperate fully with you. I'm okay with that if that little girl is missing. Where's the FBI part of this?" Deputy Sharah Hansson sat down across the conference room's oval wooden table from Al and Fergie. She plopped a file folder and notepad down in front of her.

"He's out thrashing about somewhere on his own," Al said.

"Well, I guess we can go ahead. Have you any ideas about where the girl might be?"

"Nope. It's why we're here."

"We've talked with Armand Grunderson, Eliska's father," Fergie said. "Since she may well be missing now too, along with her best friend, Gerta, this is about the only thread we have to follow."

"The FBI has a lot of resources for anything like a kidnapping," Sharah said.

"Yeah, and I hope they're using all of them." Al looked down at the file. "We're trying this one idea that maybe they aren't pursuing."

Sharah could have commented on Al not knowing exactly what the Bu guys were up to, but Al gave her credit for not saying anything about that and just opening the file.

"I was in on the questioning when rumors about Grunderson came to our attention. Her mother died in an auto accident six years ago."

"Do you think there was anything suspicious about the accident?"

"An eighteen-wheeler jackknifed into her on her way home from her job as a teacher. Anyway, he's been raising her since, perhaps questionably. That is, not physical abuse. He wasn't beating her. They like to have a female deputy handy when someone like Eliska is involved."

"I can guess about how much you got from her," Al said.

"Yep. We got nada. Of course, we got even less from Grunderson himself. He made Stonewall Jackson seem the chatty sort. All we had to go on were the concerns from neighbors and one school teacher, all of whom thought they saw differences in Eliska, the earmarks, or symptoms if you will, of some possible, I think probable, home sexual abuse. She withdrew from most of her friends, with the exception of Gerta. She alternated between defiant behavior and depression or anxiety. She had flashes of anger and hostility, and her grades were suffering."

"But you could prove nothing?" Fergie asked.

"No. Not without cooperation from Eliska herself, and she was a clam."

"How about her friend Gerta? Did you talk to her about Grunderson? Maybe he came on to her."

"Yeah, like I was going to go near that girl with a mother like she's got."

"Eliska seemed almost cocky about her involvement in that film session," Fergie said.

"And that's another tip of the iceberg that she was being rushed into physical adulthood far faster than she should have been. But we could do nothing without some corroboration."

"Can you let us copy the parts of Grunderson's file that might help us?" Al asked.

"Already done." Sharah shared a twisted grin and slid a stapled sheaf of papers to him. "If anything at all is really going on, I'd like to see this jasper go down and go down hard. Happy hunting!"

?

"These child-porn types are addicts," Fergie said. "It's just as gripping as a cocaine or meth habit. And addiction is a hard thing to understand."

Al glanced her way then looked back at the road ahead.

"What?" she said, apparently reading something in his look.

He sighed. "While Maury gets a lot of attention for his lifelong jones, chasing women, I had my own struggles back in the day."

"With what?"

"With addiction."

"Do tell."

"I whimsically took a turn at letting alcohol play a bigger part in my life."

"Really? You hardly drink at all these days."

"There's a reason for that. It took a few bounces on the head, and I gave the exercise more time than you'd think."

"You can't stop telling the story after that. I want to hear all about this."

"In one of the comic-relief early moments, I managed, as a mere boy, to steal a bottle of gin. I hid it under a juniper bush. Later, when I went back there and took a sip out of the bottle, I spit it out. It was horrible. I thought the bush had spoiled the gin's taste. I didn't know until some years later that gin tasted like that."

Fergie held a hand up to her mouth, but a chuckle got loose anyway. "You'd think that would have slowed you."

"You'd think so, but no. I switched to the usual standard of experimenting youth: beer. This was way before marijuana was going around."

"These days, I hear about grade-school kids who use such things as wild as black tar heroin," Fergie said.

"Anyway, while Maury was out steering young girls into the revolving door of the back seat of his car, I, for a spell, chose a different path. I stayed a virgin but still managed a thrill or two in my awkward childhood. I made a few buys of beer at carry-outs then grew even more daring and adventured into drinking Black Label beer in the Rathskeller pub while I was still quite underage."

"How'd you manage that?"

"I slicked my hair back with an overdose of Brylcreem and slipped on a fake wedding ring. I didn't particularly care for Black Label, but it was the first thing I saw sitting in front of another patron, so I ordered that and kind of had to stick with it. I suspected the bartender had me pegged for younger, but it was that kind of place, in the basement of a hotel."

"What happened that made you stop?"

"I just got sick of myself that way."

"That's all?"

"Well, I did have one little boost of an epiphany."

"Go on."

"There used to be this crowd of guys formerly from my high school, older than me but just barely. Still, they were legal drinkers, unlike me. I remember them pouring into the Rathskeller after an all-day bout of drinking. One of them sneaked up into the hotel kitchen and got some tomato juice so they could add that to their beer, allowing them to drink even more beer. Their taste buds had numbed, and I guess they needed to reboot them. Then they started doing shots. I recall wishing I could knock back hard liquor that way."

"Yeah, real heroic behavior."

"I thought so at the time. I mean it. I thought they were warriors, Greek gods, the true heroes and, at the same time, rascals. It gave me someone to admire, to aspire toward. Maybe I even compared them to Viking lords on a mission of conquering and gathering spoils, all overblown romantic claptrap stuff of my youth. All they really wanted to do was drink. Then I remember them all heading out in a rush to their car."

"Oh, that's a good example for you."

"Turns out it was—a harsh one. The entire lot of them were in a car that piled into the concrete abutment of a railroad bridge at an estimated seventy-five miles an hour. The reason for the estimate was because there was no one left to ask." He turned to Fergie.

She stared at him, blinked, and said, "I guess that would have made me think twice."

Chapter Seventeen

A l looked up from the file copies in his lap and stared across the lake. His left hand hung down to scratch the back of Tanner's neck. The dog sprawled along the side of the Adirondack chair and made low contented noises.

A breeze was stirring the surface of Lake Travis as far as Al could see, but it hadn't picked up enough to generate whitecaps. At the sound of footsteps approaching, Al turned his head. Fergie was coming down the flagstone path to the fishing dock. Al's bass boat swung gently on its sling in the boat dock beside him. He started to look back toward the lake, then his head snapped back to her.

She wore a white blouse tied in a knot at her midriff over shorts so short he'd have to call them Daisy Dukes. Her feet were encased in beige sandals with thin leather straps that wove up to midshin.

"You don't have to ask a penny for my thoughts," Al said.

"No, I don't. From that look, I guess I realize for the first time that you really are Maury's brother."

"Are you trying to break my chain of thought?" he asked as she settled into the matching chair next to his.

"Wouldn't dream of it. Are those the file copies you got from Deputy Hansson?"

"Yeah, those and the copies of files on Ardisson and Gibson."

"What made you want to go back through their files? I thought we were going to concentrate on Grunderson, that he was all we had."

"Something niggled."

"I went through them all."

"Yep. I know you did. Did you spot it?"

"Spot what?" Her head snapped toward him.

70

"I thought not, or you'd have said something. I wonder if Sharah did either."

"Okay, spill. You're grinning like a cat with a juicy mouse."

"Maybe not a mouse, but a lead, and at a time when fresh new leads are scarce."

"What is it? What'd you find?"

"A coincidence. It took putting two separate sheets together and sifting through the minutiae there. But it's the connection between E. Z. Ardisson and Trick Gibson, the initial connection, before it extended to the porn biz and Gerta."

"Let me see?"

He handed her the files.

She pored over each page again, flipping through them while he looked out across the water. A dock-building barge was putting along, following the edge of the far shore.

"Aw. I am an idiot. I must have looked right at it, but I went too fast the first time." She looked up from the two sheets of copy paper she held. "They both worked at the same place together some time back."

"And what a place."

"Yeah. Can you imagine those two working at a pet-rescue center?" She shook her head. The breeze sent a strand of her long red hair across her face, and she reached up to pull it away.

"Nope. I wonder if it's really a shelter or just some backwoods puppy mill, the very illegal kind."

"Or the kind of place where they are selling the pelts to black-market dealers."

When Al didn't say anything, she asked, "Are we off to go have a look at the place?"

"You bet."

?

On the way there Al said, "I haven't been to a pet-rescue center since I brought Tanner home from one."

"I know. Have you kept in touch with that woman who ran the place, Myra Henningdale?"

"I get a look from Tanner that reminds me to send in a donation every few months. That lady works some long, hard, thankless hours."

The place was as out-of-the-way as a shelter could be. A small sign out by the four-lane road directed them down a long lane that wound through some pretty rough shrubs and overgrown woods. The matching sign on the building said Happy Daze Pet Adoptions.

The sign had been the only thing to receive recent paint. The front office building was wind-sanded, weathered boards that had long ago been white. The back kennels had unpainted cinder-block walls, and some cement slabs behind the building had corrugated metal roofing slanted over open chain-link kennels.

The dogs barked and howled before Al and Fergie climbed out of his truck.

As they neared the front building, Al began to smell the cats, the rich perfume of musky ammonia. Fergie's nose twitched—kind of hard to miss a smell like that.

The barking increased in intensity until it became a nearly hysterical wave. A beat-up blue Ford Ranger was parked near the office. Only one other car, a white Jeep Cherokee, was pulled up close to the building, but no other cars filled the gravel parking lot. Al doubted a lot of people drove all the way from Austin to look over the pets.

They were almost to the front door when it opened. A woman led a leashed dog that looked to Al like a whippet or one of those greyhounds retired from its track running days. Instead of springing around on its long spindly legs, it seemed to sulk, tail down, doing its best not to look at Al or Fergie.

The woman didn't seem to mind. She dragged him along, the leash straight out behind her. "Come on, Bootsie," she said.

The brindle dog had legs that were white from midshin down to his paws.

The man standing in the doorway might have been grinning, but that was hard for Al to tell. He had a day or two of rough stubble on his face. He wore tired-looking jeans and a flannel shirt with large red, white, and black checks. Its sleeves were cut off at the shoulders, revealing thick, hairy upper arms and a faded tattoo that could have been either a mermaid with a dagger going through it, or a ship going down at sea.

He saw Al and Fergie and nearly managed a smile, one that faltered and didn't quite stick its landing.

"Welcome to Happy Daze," he said, swinging the door open wide.

Al had turned to watch the lady wrestle her reluctant dog into the back of the Cherokee. He had spread his legs, and she had to give a shove to pop him in.

"Are you interested in picking up a fur pal?"

Al turned back to the guy, who was trying hard.

"Oliver Minsky. Call me Ollie. Come on in."

Al and Fergie followed the man inside. They passed an open office off to the right, where a thin blond woman about the same age as Minsky looked up at them. She seemed too hard at the edges to be frail.

"That's Reba, the wife. You can't adopt her, though it would save me money if you did." He made a rumbling sound that was probably intended to be a laugh.

"Now, let me see. Dogs or cats?"

"Dogs," Al said.

Minsky led the way through open rooms with cages and travel crates filled with dogs of all breeds, mostly mixed. They barked in an excited cacophony, from deep booms to sharp yips. Some howled, and others joined in.

Without looking back, Minsky took a couple of blue earplugs out of his front shirt pocket and jammed them into his ears. "Let me know if you see anything you like."

The dogs all looked fairly dirty and unkempt to Al, who gave Tanner a good soapy scrubbing in the shower at least once a month.

"Do you have a lot of other people who work for you," Al asked, "or is it just the two of you?"

"I've taken on help from time to time, but you know..." He held a hand out flat and wiggled his fingers. "They come. They go."

He opened the door to a much-bigger back room, and dogs in kennels lining both sides went hysterical, banging metal food bowls and clanging around while barking and leaping at the kennel doors.

Talking was out of the question in the back room. Al glanced toward Fergie. She looked as though she wouldn't say no to a pair of earplugs, even the ones Minsky would have to take out of his own ears.

Minsky paused in front of a kennel now and then to wave at a dog inside. Only one or two of them looked as though they wanted to tear Al or Fergie apart. Then he led them out a back door to where the kennels were chain-link fencing surrounding concrete slabs.

The barking and leaping about was just as intense outside but slightly more tolerable since the cinderblock walls of the enclosed kennels weren't magnifying the sound.

The fur of most of the dogs was matted. Their nails were long. Al supposed they got a grooming if someone was coming to look at a specific dog, but no one had spent a great deal of time with a brush on any of those dogs.

They had gone right by a large room filled with cats, but Al could see an outside caged extension of that area where thirty or so cats moved around or lounged on shelves.

To one side, a new slab of concrete had been poured. Some steel posts and a coil of chain-link fence lay next to it. The place seemed about full and was still growing.

"How many pets do you have?" Fergie asked.

"Eighty-six dogs and a hundred and twenty-seven cats. One less if you choose to take one home today."

"We're just looking for now," she said, which seemed to take a little air out of Minsky.

He moved them through the rest of their tour quickly. Soon, they stood in the hallway outside the office, which was open to the hallway as a reception area.

"Are you sure you don't want to take a fur pal home?" Minsky asked. "Mopsy back there took a real shine to you."

Al couldn't recall which one had been Mopsy. They had all looked like a pretty hardscrabble lot of mutts. Then again, even his Tanner had a questionable mix of parentage.

"You sure you showed them every dog that might be right for them?" Reba sat in a chair facing an office desk. She looked to be the sparkplug of the place, though even as she spoke, she seemed tired, as though she was forcing herself to be cheerful.

"They're just looking," Minsky said.

Al could have read that as "just snooping." *Oh well, if the gloves are off.* He asked, "Do you recall a guy named E. Z. Ardisson? Used to work for you."

Minsky glanced toward his wife.

"Sure we do," she said in a voice with a squeaky rasp. "We read in the papers where he came to a messy end. Didn't surprise me. He was a little too eager to make his pile, and soon, and that usually bites a young man in the butt."

Al could have said that being slashed to ribbons by a knife was hardly a bite in the butt.

"Or Trick Gibson?" Fergie said.

"Nasty ending for him as well." Reba shook her head. "Young men these days. Who knows all they're into?"

Minsky's eyes narrowed, and Al figured they had used up all the courtesy time they dared. Al gave Fergie's elbow a nudge, and they headed out the door. The barking faded behind them as they climbed into his truck.

Al said, "Something does smell a little."

"And not just in a starkly literal way." Fergie closed her door. "Let's just follow this thread and see where it takes us."

Chapter Eighteen

As he drove back out the lane, Al took out his cell phone and made the call, getting someone he knew at the sheriff's department.

"Hey, Mavis. It's Al Quinn here. Can you run a license-plate number for me?"

"Are you active again?"

"Clayton thinks I am."

"Okay then." In a moment, she gave him an address a lot farther away from the shelter than he would have guessed. "The plate's for a Candice Dowell," Mavis said. "I'm guessing she lives alone, from the way her number is listed. No mister and missus, that sort of thing."

He hung up and glanced toward Fergie. "It's a ways for someone to go to get a pooch, but it's in the county."

Al drove for nearly thirty miles through traffic that was only beginning to tie itself into knots as rush hour approached. He pulled up in front of a neighborhood house on the far outskirts of Austin. The house was meant to look like a log cabin, dark brown except for expanses of bright white quartzite, which along with the two-car garage, complied with the area's zoning ordinances. Every house had to be one-quarter stone or brick.

"You know we had to drive right past another pet-rescue center to get here," Fergie said as she got out of the truck.

"Yep. It's why we're here."

The lawn was nicely kept and had been recently mowed. Red and yellow sweet-potato vines spilled out of two large pots on either side of the front door.

Al rang the doorbell.

Fergie stood beside him, looking over the lawn. "My bet is she has a guy come by to do the yard work each week."

When the door swung open, Al asked, "Candice Dowell?"

In the background a dog barked—Bootsie, no doubt.

The woman looked them over, perhaps to determine whether they were selling something. Her once-blond hair was going to grey, and she was letting it. Just guessing, Al would have figured her for a retired schoolteacher.

"Do you have a moment?" Fergie asked. "We'd like to ask about the dog you adopted."

"How did you know about that?" Her head tilted as her eyes narrowed.

"We had just pulled into the lot as you were leaving with Bootsie," Fergie said.

"You're thinking about getting a dog?"

"Sure," Al said. "We wanted to ask you about the process."

"Well, that part's easy enough. You might as well come in, but don't let the dog jump up on you. I'm still trying to get him settled down. New home and all."

Inside, Bootsie was living up to his past, if he was indeed a greyhound, by running around and around the couch, love seat, and coffee table facing the big-screen television against the far wall.

"He'll wear down in time." Candice turned her head to watch him do another lap. His tongue was hanging out, but Al couldn't tell if he was happy or making an imaginary escape in his head.

"He's probably tickled at having some freedom after living in a kennel for a while," Fergie said.

"You'd think so." She looked up from where the dog was still doing laps. "It's the deal you want to know about, isn't it?"

"The deal?" Fergie asked.

"I heard about it from a friend in my book club."

"Heard about what?" Al said.

"I'll show you." She picked up a folder lying on the coffee table. She went through it and pulled out a paper, which she held out to them.

The adoption paper looked normal and straightforward to Al. He'd signed one to take Tanner home.

Fergie pointed to a box in the upper right-hand corner. It was for the adoption fee, and the amount was fifteen hundred dollars.

"You paid fifteen hundred for Bootsie?" Al asked.

"You see, that's the thing. The deal. They have to put something there, but that nice man waived the fee. They're so happy to place the dogs, I guess."

"I guess so." Fergie looked at Al.

Al watched Bootsie run around and around the room, relentlessly, probably burning off some energy from being in a new home. At least he would get a chance to settle in, be treated fairly, get fed, get walked, be washed and combed, have treats, and be petted—

quite a change from the conditions Al had seen at Happy Daze. Almost every one of the people he'd met in pet-rescue centers wanted to do good. People like the Minskys didn't feel right somehow.

Minutes later, walking back out to the truck, Al asked, "You see a place showing money coming in but not really getting it, what's the first thing you think?"

"Money laundering. I know it was a big deal for a while in the night spots because with people coming and going, who's to say if the night's revenues are what the club reports. But a pet-rescue center—that's new to me."

"Let's visit a couple of my friends in the biz," Al said.

He turned on the AC and let it run for a few moments before they climbed back into his truck. The day was heating up.

To keep from fighting Austin rush-hour traffic, he drove his truck out and around the city's edge as much as he could.

Forty minutes later, Fergie and Al walked back through the pet-rescue center Myra Henningdale ran, a barking gauntlet of dogs in kennels on either side. They found her hosing out kennels while the dogs played in the yard. She put the hose aside and closed the kennel doors. As soon as she smiled, she looked as young and spry as a teenager. With long dark hair and somewhat-sad hazel eyes, she looked tired but fulfilled.

When people in their forties looked as young as she did to Al, he always wondered just how old he was getting himself, but he didn't let himself dwell on it.

"Let me get Buster and Hops back in their kennels, and we can talk," she said over the sound of barking all around them.

Once the dogs were in the kennels, she led Al and Fergie to her office, her rubber boots squeaking with each step. She pulled off the rubber gloves she wore and tossed them onto the desk.

"Don't tell me you've come hoping to turn Tanner back in to us," she said.

"I won't. He has a permanent home." Al turned to Fergie. "Right?"

"Yep. He's family. Al and I were never able to have children."

Al felt his face flush all the way back to his ears, but Myra chuckled. She seemed to know Fergie was just joshing.

"I wanted to ask you about adoption fees. Do you waive them sometimes?" Al asked.

She nodded. "If the situation calls for it. I figure if a somewhat needy family is willing to give a pet a home and feed it, the least I can do is pitch in."

"What's the usual adoption fee?" Fergie asked.

"What Al paid. Eighty dollars. But it can vary. Even then, it hardly pays for the heavy vet bills some of them run up and the regular costs of rabies shots, neutering or spaying, and getting them chipped. Not to mention feeding some of them for quite a spell."

Al didn't bring up the fact that Tanner had been only a couple of days away from being euthanized because of his age in an overcrowded shelter.

"What would you say to someone charging fifteen hundred as an adoption fee?" Fergie asked.

"I'd say they were crazy."

"You ever hear of a guy named Oliver Minsky?" Al asked.

"Oh. Him and his Happy Daze place. Sure, I've heard of him before. He even stopped around in the past. Said he'd be willing to take any pets off my hands if I was overcrowded."

"What'd you say?"

"I said no. Sounded fishy on the face of it. I've turned labs over to the lab-rescue people before and wiener dogs to the wiener-dog people. Maybe he's on some kind of 501C nonprofit plan where he needs numbers. But I figure he can get pets the regular way. Plenty of people surrender them or are outlived by them. He's not the one charging fifteen hundred, is he?"

Fergie nodded.

"Well, maybe it does make sense him wanting pets if he's getting that for them."

Al figured Myra was piled high with work as usual, and he'd gotten all he could from her. He turned and headed for the center's front door, with Fergie right behind him.

As they walked back to Al's truck, Fergie said, "But the thing is he isn't getting that for them if he's waiving the fees."

"Still smells funny to me," Al said.

The truck's door was hot to his touch. Once again, he had to give the AC a chance to make the cab tolerable before they climbed in.

Next, he drove to a shelter run by the lanky redhead Taylor James. He had been part of a case Al had worked a while back.

Al enjoyed the drive more, beginning to savor the notion they were onto something. He glanced toward Fergie, who grinned back at him.

They found James in a small quarantine room, sitting on the floor with a litter of eight lab puppies clambering all over his legs and tugging at the bottom of his shirt. Sometimes, the hardworking folks at rescue centers did have fun.

He brushed them off, stood, and slipped out the door. Al peeked in through the door's window at them climbing all over each other. Some were white, two were black, and the others were a reddish brown.

"All the same mother," said James. "Can you believe it? And she's a chocolate lab named Mocha."

They had their chat in the hallway outside the room full of puppies.

"Yeah, the guy came to me about being willing to take any over-flow," James said. "I do everything here, even what vet work I can. I sent him packing. I've got people lined up to take the pets I care for. And mind you, I vet them closely so they are committed to treating the pets as part of the family. A dog isn't a goldfish. If I hear someone's tying one of mine up and leaving it in their yard, I'll be after them to give it back. I hear that Minsky guy doesn't ask questions and would put a dog in a bag and let you go out the door with it."

When they got to the part about the adoption fees, James burst out laughing so hard Al didn't think he would be able to stop. He slapped a knee. "Fifteen hundred! You have got to be kidding. Go ahead, tell me you're kidding."

Chapter Nineteen

"What is it you think you have?" Clayton leaned back in his office chair and looked across his desk at Fergie and Al.

"A connection," Al said, "between the late E. Z. Ardisson and Trick Gibson and a pet-rescue center, Happy Daze."

"I know about that. Victor spotted that too and mentioned it. He thought it was a coincidence."

"Even if the place is shady?" Fergie asked.

"Shady how?"

"Money laundering, we think," Fergie said.

Clayton's large head swung toward Fergie. "Back when you were a detective for the city police department, did you ever go into Lieutenant Strummers's office and give him anything as unsubstantiated and flimsy to go on? You know, something the public and the press would call a witch hunt?"

"No." Fergie didn't blink. "That's why Al and I did a little homework before coming to your office."

"The place has a current population of two hundred and thirteen pets," Al said. "The adoption paper we saw said the adoption fee for a dog is fifteen hundred dollars."

"What?" Clayton sat up straight in his chair.

"But the adopters don't have to pay the fee. Word is, it'll be waived every time," Fergie said. "Yet the Happy Daze center posted an income of over a quarter of a million dollars last year and included on its payroll a number of paid staff."

"That included E. Z. Ardisson and Trick Gibson, both with ties to the porn biz, and by that, I mean kiddie porn," Al said.

"We're not even sure whether they worked there or just drew a paycheck from the place. As Victor apparently pointed out, they both claimed it as a past employer." Fergie slid a manila folder across the desk to Clayton. "But them knowing about the place, and about any money laundering that might be going through it, could have been what got them killed."

Clayton didn't reach for the file right away. Instead, he frowned. "You know what a righteous pain it is to get a search warrant for something like this, right?"

Al waited.

"And if we don't find hard evidence, it's going to leave us with egg on my face."

"What are you saying?" Fergie asked.

"I'm thinking you are already working hand-in-hand with the FBI."

"Are you saying we should let them have all the thunder on this?"

"I'm hinting rather firmly in that direction."

"But they don't give a whoop about finding Gerta. All I'm trying to accomplish here is to get any kind of lead to where she might be."

"Okay, then you can be there too. But do this together."

"Really? You think that's possible?" Al said.

"What I intend is for you to work together. You get what you want, and Aaron gets what he wants. *Capisce?*"

"I wish I could be as confident as you that he'll plan on playing fair."

"I'll have your warrant by noon tomorrow. Meet Victor Kahlon here, and you'll be good to go. He'll round up a few deputies to help with the search. Now, I'll just give Aaron a heads-up."

He was reaching for the phone as Al and Fergie stood and left the room.

?

Rain was pouring as hard as it ever could in Texas when Al pulled his truck into the department parking lot barely half an hour after noon the next day.

They got out of Al's truck and splashed their way across the lot to climb into the back of Victor Kahlon's cruiser.

"This is Bennie." Victor nodded toward the deputy in the front passenger seat. "He's one of our number-crunching fellas, the way Meat Jenkins does our tech stuff."

Al knew Meat Jenkins, but Bennie was new to him, as probably more than half the sheriff's department staff was since his retirement. They made him feel as if he had been gone for more years than he really had been.

Another cruiser pulled out behind them in rain so thick and hard that Al had a hard time seeing the yellow stripe along its coppery side as it moved out onto the street.

"How many deputies are you bringing along?"

"Four more in that car, and two of them have K-9 experience if we come to need any of that. That's all Clayton would spare for this goose chase of yours." He glanced at Al in the rearview mirror. "Not that I think it's a waste of time. Your notions have always paid off handsomely for me. I may make lieutenant in only a couple or three more years."

When Al didn't say anything, Victor turned his wipers up to a higher speed and asked, "You ever think of doing this on a sunny day?"

"It was sunny yesterday," Al said.

The rest of the ride was quiet except for the growl of the tires rasping and splashing along the road.

"Oh, my great-aunt Fanny's fanny," Victor muttered. He pulled the cruiser into the gravel parking lot outside Happy Daze after going down the long lane.

Three black SUVs were parked in a row outside the front building.

As soon as Victor and his fellow deputies, along with Fergie and Al, spilled out of their cars to stand dripping in the rain, four heavily armed men, complete with helmets, vests and Heckler & Koch MP5s, rushed up to them. The "FBI" across their vests eliminated the need for any questions.

They didn't raise their weapons at the deputies, but they did block the way in.

"Where's Aaron Masterson?" Victor asked.

One of them nodded toward the back.

The only satisfaction Al got out of the brief confrontation was knowing those guys were getting as wet as he was.

Victor led the way around back. Al reached over to nudge him, then pointed toward the slab of the unfinished new kennel. Aaron stood on it, directing three other agents, who moved through the kennels and checked the grounds all the way to the distant back fence. The dogs were barking hysterically.

"What the hell are you doing?" Al yelled, barely hearing himself above the din of the rain and barking dogs.

Victor held Al's elbow to keep him from rushing forward.

Aaron turned his head toward Al, nodded toward the front office, and took off walking in that direction. The men outside continued searching.

Aaron went inside through the back kennel door, and the others followed.

Al tried to speak as they passed through the kennels on both sides, but the barking was too fierce and intense. He doubted if the dogs had ever been subjected to that many strangers passing right through their kennels.

As soon as Al, Fergie, and Victor, along with his other deputies, closed the door to the kennels behind them, Aaron said, "Here's where it gets interesting."

All the deputies, even the ones with K-9 experience, were rubbing their ears or shaking their heads after passing through the kennels, where the noise was bounced around by the cinder-block walls.

Aaron led the way up to the front office. "We called in our own ME but will be getting reports to your department as soon as we know all we can know."

Oliver Minsky lay on his back just inside the front door. His eyes were bloody holes with blackened edges. *Bing. Bing.* The entry wounds looked small to Al, like what a .22 would make.

Reba lay sprawled on her back on the office floor, a small pool of blood congealing around the spray of her blond hair, which fanned out on the tiles.

"Are their MOs consistent?" Al asked.

"We'll know for sure after the ME finishes. But at first blush, it looks exactly the same to me. Someone held the woman down and did her first. When the guy came in, he caught one in one eye, and the job was finished on the floor, even if the second shot wasn't necessary. It would seem to be some sort of message," Aaron said.

"And you haven't found anything in the files, no caches of money on the grounds?" Al thought of the warrant in Victor's shirt pocket, a warrant they wouldn't get to use.

"No money, unless you count a petty-cash drawer of less than twelve dollars. We're sending everything else back to the lab to see what they can make of it there. What there is left of it."

"What's that mean?" Al asked.

Aaron sighed. "It means this." He led Al and Fergie to the room across from the office. Smaller crates and kennels lined the walls, and the dogs whipped up into an even greater fury at the intruders.

Along the back wall, where bag after bag of dog food and cat food had been stored on shelves, someone had ripped out the wall, shelves and all, and had piled the bags of food out of the way, spilling out into the crowded center of the room. Some bags had burst open as they had been tossed aside. The mice were going to have a field day once they found all that.

The several feet behind where the wall had been was an empty space.

"You think that's where money was stored, a great bulky amount of it?" Al asked.

"I don't think anything for sure, yet. Our guys have ways of checking to make sure what was stored here and is now gone. But yes, I suspect they may find it was money. In fact, I'm almost certain of it."

"And the people who did the Minskys knew about it and took it?" Fergie asked.

"Everything is speculation at this point. Like I said, Clayton will get a report."

"Did you find anything that might lead us to the missing girls, Gerta in particular?"

"Not a thing... yet. We'll let you know if we do come across anything."

"I thought we were working together."

"You'll get a copy of any intel we come across. But I've got to tell you, I took a glance through the files, and it doesn't look promising."

"No empty files where anything was taken?"

Aaron shrugged. "Hard to tell what cabinets were once full or always half-empty."

"No ties to other locations? There would have to be a number of places like this if they were laundering money for the likes of the sort of operation we're talking about."

"That's a big if. We haven't found anything yet that confirms any laundering. We'll let you know if and when we do." Aaron's words were starting to take on a crisp edge.

"Well, I doubt if it was a disappointed pet adopter who came in and finished off the Minskys in as professional-looking a hit as I've seen in a while."

"As I said," Aaron was talking through his teeth, "we'll let you know what we find out. Wait for the report."

Al looked at Fergie. She shook her head, knowing he had to be boiling inside, but that wasn't the time or place.

"What are you going to do about all these pets?" Al asked.

For the first time, Aaron cracked a hearty grin. "That's a job for the county—sheriff's department, probably."

?

Al waited until they were back out in the cruisers before he made the call to Clayton. They sat in the cars, damp and discouraged and smelling like wet sheep. Fergie had begun to shiver. Al nodded to Victor to start the engine and get the heater going.

"Aaron was here with a full team, as well as an ME working the double homicide," he growled into his cellphone.

"Well, I guess you'd better bring our folks home, then, if the Bu is already all over this. I'll damn well let them deal with the media, too."

"I wonder if I might use the men with me for a chore."

Clayton had to know how steamed Al was about Aaron's jumping the gun. After a pause of heavy silence from Al, he asked, "What?"

"There are over two hundred pets here. Someone's either got to care for them here, or we could move them to some of the other shelters in the county. I know a number of the people who run those shelters."

"I don't think that'll hurt anything. I'll send over our animal control people as well."

He hung up, and Al put his phone away.

"What did you get us into this time, Al?" Victor asked.

"Smile," Al said. "You've just been promoted to dogcatcher."

?

Al sat on the end of his bed, rubbing Tanner behind the ears. "We sure got some of your fur buddies moved about today," he said.

Fergie came out of the bathroom after her shower. She had one large gray towel wrapped around her and was rubbing her hair dry with a smaller matching one.

"How do you feel?" she asked.

"Wet and half-chilled all the way through despite having a shower and a warm bowl of soup," he said. "And I'm tired and still a little bit angry."

"Do you ever wonder why you still do detective work at your age?"

"I'd rather that than be one of those guys who used to be a television sidekick but now does commercials and opens shopping malls."

"Or some one-hit-wonder pop-chart singer from way back who's doomed to sing the same song over and over until he's your age."

He could have mentioned that she was the same age, but he didn't. "Yeah, that too," he said.

"Well, what do we do now? Gerta's still out there somewhere, and we didn't get a step closer to her." Fergie rubbed harder at her hair with the towel then reached up to separate red strands of it.

"We're right back where we were going before this quite unproductive distraction," he said.

"Grunderson?"

"Yeah. But tomorrow. Tonight, we sleep."

"Maybe." She dropped the large towel to the floor. "But not right away."

Chapter Twenty

The Bone Lady stepped up to the hanging side of beef. Al felt Fergie move close and press her thigh and left arm against him. She flinched when the Bone Lady lifted her long knife and sliced deep into the meat. The knife clicked against bone when the blade stopped. Blood oozed out of the far back of the slice. Fergie shuddered delicately.

"Tha's the jelly," the Bone Lady said. "It means I'm at the joint, where I should be."

She put her knife down and picked up a large hacksaw and sawed away at the bone. She caught the lower portion of beef when it fell away, cradling it in one arm while she put the saw down. She carried the slab over to a table and put it down on one side. Then she reached for her knife and started cutting away some fat.

Al could see the tenderloin nestled along the inside of the spine.

The Bone Lady used short feathering slices, running the tip of her knife between the meat and bone to loosen the cut of meat and fiddle it out of the steer.

Al hadn't ever thought of it before, but that was a filleting move, just the same as what he used when cleaning fish—hence, *filet mignon.*

The Bone Lady lifted the tenderloin out, trimmed away most of the fat, and put the meat on a tray. The young man who was standing by in his white butcher-shop outfit stepped in and whisked the cut away, carrying it toward the front, to a waiting customer.

"Tenderest cut in a beef, but I won' have none of it. There's a lot more taste in other cuts."

Fergie eased back away from touching his side now that the butchering was over and the Bone Lady had put down her knife.

91

"Wha' I wanna know is why is it taking so long?" She shook her head. "You know that each day she's away..."

"We try not to think of things like that, or at least not focus on them," Fergie said. "It's best not to. We're working as fast as we can. There's just been very little trail to follow."

The Bone Lady's gaze stayed fixed on Al. "You sure you're up to this? Everyone I know said you were tops."

Al had been dreading the visit, and Fergie even more so. He'd had a glimmer of a lead that had merely turned into two fresh bodies, not to mention a meddlesome FBI agent who had done doodley-squat toward helping Al find Gerta.

He was disappointed in himself and felt he'd taken a wrong turn and wasted time that was indeed precious, as the Bone Lady pointed out. He didn't share that with her, though. The chance that Gerta would never be found or would be found dead or damaged increased with every moment.

Al knew not to hang his head. He looked straight into her un-flinching eyes. "We will do this and get her back to you if it can be done. We will do everything we possibly can."

She nodded and turned to pick up her knife, clean it under a faucet, and sharpen it on a stone as they turned and headed out of the shop.

?

"Scoot over, buddy. I need to keep a watch here." Al gently moved Tanner from his lap over to Fergie's. She put an arm around Tanner to hold him in place. With her other hand, she rubbed him behind his ears and down the fluffy nape of his neck. With Maury and Bonnie both in the hospital, they'd wanted to bring him along. Where they were sitting, Al had a clear image of a house through his binoculars.

The rising full moon had both helped Al and made him nervous at the same time as he had eased his truck up Grunderson's lane with his lights off. The house being tucked into the woods helped as well. He was able to back into and among the trees and shrubs until the branch-es of a thick copse of sumac and mountain cedar hid his truck.

"We're lucky he isn't one of those groomed-lawn-and-landscaped-property types," Fergie had said.

Still, Al hoped no flicker of color from his truck would show through if Grunderson decided to leave his house.

What lights were on in the house revealed only one tall figure in the house, most often sitting but sometimes roaming—restlessly, it seemed to Al. No smaller figure was present.

"Eliska Grunderson. Where the hell are you, Eliska? And Gerta along with you?"

After three solid hours of watching as the night got darker around them, Al finally watched Grunderson stir from his chair and turn out all but one light. Moments later, the garage door opened, and Grunder-son's car, a BMW, pulled out.

Even though he didn't believe Grunderson could spot his truck through the thick limbs that surrounded it, especially if he was think-ing of something else, Al and Fergie both ducked as the beams of head-lights swept over their hiding place.

Al followed at a safe distance. He'd seen enough of Grunderson to suspect the man might just be paranoid enough to keep an eye out for a tail, especially if he had a guilty conscience.

Some eleven and a half miles later, the BMW swung into the park-ing lot of a coffee shop standing alone in a growing suburban neighbor-hood. A few other shops were in a strip mall next to it, but all of them were closed.

Al went around the block, giving Grunderson time to get out of his car and go inside. Then he scouted the parking lot until he found the ideal place to back into, where the truck sat in the shadow of the drooping limbs of a live oak, yet Al could see inside. With the binoc-ulars, he watched Grunderson pick up a mug at the counter and carry it over to a table. The man didn't take out his cell phone or even look around much.

"The FBI may well have his phone tapped. Even if they don't, he'll be wary that they might." Fergie held out a hand. "Let me have a look."

She adjusted the binoculars while Tanner squirmed in her lap. Al kept him calm with a slow belly rub.

"He's just sitting there." She handed the glasses back to Al.

Madrigal Joe's Coffee Shop had a bit of a reputation for being a gay-friendly place, yet Al guessed eighty percent of their business came from locals and those who merely wanted a quiet place to drop in and have a good cup of coffee with a scone while peering into their laptops or cell phones. The rainbow banner and flag outside just added color to another authentic and original business on the outskirts of Austin. It had been a bit of a drive for Grunderson to go all the way into town from his place, which gave Al the ray of hope that kept them camped outside in the darkness that had settled over the city like a tight pair of black nylon hose.

"He's still sitting there but looking around more," Al said. "No. Wait. He just got slowly to his feet. He's going over to the bookshelf on the left as you go inside the door. His eyes aren't on the books. He's watching the other patrons. Now he's sliding over to the bulletin board. Bingo! Looks like he's tacking a white three-by-five card in among the other ads and announcements. His hands are shaking. Now he's headed back to his seat."

"We still have to wait, right?"

"Yeah. I want to see if anyone goes to it after he leaves."

The next three-quarters of an hour crawled excruciatingly along. Finally, Grunderson stood and headed for the door. He didn't pause outside but went right for his car. In moments, his taillights faded away until they were out of sight. Al, Fergie, and Tanner waited.

Not a single person approached the bulletin board while they watched. The barista, a tall, lean fellow with his long hair done up in a bun, never came out from behind the counter, spending any free time between filling cups with cleaning the kitchen and urns around him for what would be another long, caffeine-rich day for patrons the next day.

"I'd better go in and get a couple of coffees to go," Fergie said. "They're about to close."

While she was gone, Tanner curled up on the spot where she'd been sitting.

Fergie snapped a photo of the card with her phone in the barest pause as she came back out to the truck.

She handed him a coffee, put hers into the console holder, and peered into the screen of her phone. She enlarged the picture then looked up and shook her head. "We're going to need some help with this. It's in some sort of code."

"Of course it is," Al said. "That's good."

"How is that good?"

"Because people who use codes have something worth hiding."

?

Al pulled his truck into the gravel parking lot of Madrigal Joe's Coffee Shop twenty minutes before it opened at 7:00 a.m. He again backed the truck into the deep shade of the same live oak tree whose limbs hung over the edge of the lot from a neighboring back yard. From there, he could see in through a picture window to the ordering counter, where two people were futzing about as they prepped to open.

The moment one of them crossed to unlock the door and swing it wide for the half-dozen patrons already waiting for their caffeine-and-pastry fix, he said, "You're on."

Fergie slid out the door on her side and crunched across the gravel to the door.

She came back to the truck a few minutes later holding two to-go cups of coffee. "The card's gone," she said as she slid back into her side of the front seat.

"What do you mean?"

"It's not on the bulletin board where it was when the place closed last night. Did you see any of the first customers go to the board or take it?"

"No."

"Then what...?"

"It's gotta be someone on the inside. Let's go."

They put their cups into the console beverage holders and stepped back out into a morning that was already approaching the temperature of freshly popped toast.

On the pretext of buying a couple of bear claws, Al asked the barista, whose name was Fred, according to the name embroidered above the pocket on his shirt, "Anyone know what happened to a three-by-five file card that was on the bulletin board last night but isn't there now?"

"You couldn't prove anything by me. I don't even glance at that board. People could be selling elephants, for all I know or care."

"But the card...?"

Fred shrugged. "They come and go."

"Well, this one went. Is there anyone else who may know anything about it?"

"Just the night shift. Only one person shuts down, and that's Ian."

"Ian who?"

"Ian Burkov."

"Where's he live?"

"I can't tell you that. Besides, he's probably home sleeping just now."

Al took his bag of bear claws, and Fergie followed along outside.

She had her phone out and was typing away. "Today's phone book—any search engine that's handy. Ah, there it is. One of the few people left with a landline. He doesn't live all that far from here."

They walked up to the front of the Tortoise Hills apartments, the sort of barely maintained cluster where, mostly, students willing to ride a bus a long while to the University of Texas campus dwelled. Number

407 was all the way down on the right, on the first floor, the next-to-last apartment.

Al rapped on the door. It sounded hollow as a drum. They waited. Nothing.

On a whim, he started around the side of the building. At the back, each tiny apartment had a small deck of a porch with a waist-high white wooden railing. The back door to Ian's apartment stood a foot open.

"Uh-oh," Fergie said. She reached down and took the S&W Chief's Special out of her ankle holster, the main reason she was wearing jeans on such a warm day.

Al nudged the door open with his shoulder, not touching any of its surfaces with his hands.

Fergie went in first with her gun. "Clear," she called back. "Very clear. As clear as it gets."

Al eased into the apartment. It was indeed a tiny one. A kitchenette ran along one wall next to the door to the bathroom. The fridge and the range were combined into one half-sized appliance. The phone hung on the wall to one side of the kitchenette. The rest was one room with a mattress on the floor, only partially covered by a rumpled sheet.

Al put a hand inside the tail of his shirt and used it to open the fridge. Its light shone on empty, off-white walls inside.

"Oh, how the rich do live these days," he said.

A nearly empty liter bottle of cheap white wine sat on the floor by what was probably the head of the bed. An open-mouthed jar that had once held applesauce was serving as the crystal stemware.

Fergie opened the door to the room's one small closet. Only three bent hangers dangled from the closet rod. On one of them hung what looked like a worn and worthless pair of jeans. A spot rubbed in the dust of the closet floor showed where a piece of luggage or duffel bag had rested.

"If I had to guess," Fergie said, "I'd say this guy is in the wind. I wonder what sent a breeze up his skirt?"

"I'm betting it was whatever was on that card. He must have been a link in some sort of line of communication, one that is closed for business now."

"I guess we'd better figure out what the scribbles on that card meant, and we're going to need some special help for that."

"Oh dear God," Fergie said. "Not Meat Jenkins."

"He's the only one who comes to mind."

"Maybe we should stop and get some nose plugs or Vicks Vaporub like you rub inside your nose while watching someone do an autopsy."

"His particular blend of halitosis and BO is of vintage and potent proportions. Maybe we can manage the whole conversation outdoors," Al said.

"And upwind if possible."

They slipped out the door and headed back around the apartment building toward the truck.

Chapter Twenty-one

Al pulled up in front of Meat Jenkins's yellow house, which stood all alone in the middle of his large lot, up a long gravel lane from the two-lane road. It was an introvert's dream palace.

He turned to Fergie. "Do you want to stay in the truck?"

"As much as I would rather avoid someone who thinks personal hygiene is an abstract concept that doesn't apply to him, I'd better come too."

The door swung open at Al's knock.

"Hey, Al," said Meat. "How'd you know I'd be home?"

"You know Al," Fergie said. "He told me that when he used to travel down to the coast for fishing trips, he always knew the tide tables and timed his visits accordingly. When it comes to needing high-level tech support, he keeps the same sort of eye on your work schedule at the sheriff's department. So he knew you'd be home."

"That's sure Al for you."

"How's the diet coming, Meat?"

"It's getting the best of me in three falls." He patted his round belly. "How's that passel of folks you've got staying at your place?"

"Well, two of them are in the hospital at the moment."

"Sounds like I'm doing better with my so-called diet than you are with tending to your crowd."

Al nodded and managed a grin despite having just caught a good whiff of Meat's particular odor, which after a previous visit, Fergie had claimed could be weaponized.

"Come on inside." Meat waved an arm of his gray sweatshirt, which also served as a handkerchief when his nose was runny. He wore yellow rumpled pants and loafers without socks. His teeth showed brightly white in a grin surrounded by his thick black beard.

Al stayed standing on the doormat. He could see empty potato-chip bags and soda cans on the carpet inside. "We've just a moment or two."

"Is this about the thing you e-mailed me?"

"Yeah. What did you make of it?" Al asked.

"I didn't make anything out of it. It's encrypted as well as anything I've ever seen."

"Not a dent, eh?"

Meat shook his head. "I'll tell you who's good with this sort of thing."

"Let me guess. The FBI?"

"You've got it. On that subject, you know I had to send something like this on to Clayton."

"Did you, now?"

"Yeah. After the last time I helped you with a techie sort of wrinkle in one of your cases, he asked to be kept in the loop. And don't you know, he passed on a message that he'd like you to drop by. Pronto, he said."

"Well, thanks worlds, Meat."

"I do what I can to spread joy and goodness all about."

?

Al and Fergie were ushered into Clayton's office an hour and a half later by a deputy who again seemed far too young to Al. He wondered if the stiff-backed young fellow even shaved yet. That was just another earmark of getting on in years enough to be retired, not that he got much opportunity to lounge around at home and enjoy those leisure hours.

"I thought I asked you to work with that FBI guy," Clayton said while Al and Fergie were still easing themselves into chairs across from him. Several stacks of files cluttered his large desk, but he leaned back in his chair for a moment to glower at Al.

"He was kind of an asshole," Al said.

"You've worked with assholes before. Hell, I can be one myself from time to time."

Al knew better than to respond to that.

"Look, this guy's bosses, all the way up as far as they go, know he's a bit eager, a potential loose cannon. But they're watching him and steering him, alternating with giving him a loose leash at other times when he needs it. That's part of growth. It's like parenting at a professional level."

"I would have hoped he'd have been all the way grown up by now."

"At any rate, they say he's on the fast track. J. Edgar Hoover himself was probably like this once."

"I just don't want his tracks going up one side of me and down the other. I've had that experience before with some feds. Didn't care for it."

"Just do what you do. Work your wonders in mysterious ways to deliver as you usually do."

"Why not use some of your regular detectives? Victor Kahlon seems a good one."

"His penny is shining particularly bright, but that's mainly because you put a few cases right into his lap."

"You don't think he's any part of a leak, do you?"

"What makes you think there's a leak?"

"Everything about the way you're handling this."

"Al, you know a case like this may be teetering on the edge of something so much bigger if it's worth killing people over and bribing others. There could be millions at stake and a great need to buy information and a firewall to keep people like us out. I have a huge department of carefully vetted people. But hardly any of them feel they're making the kind of money they deserve. There's always going to be an element of temptation."

"And this Aaron fellow?"

"I've already sent the information you found on to him. He says he'll let you know the moment their cryptography people crack the code. So, for the moment, I suggest you sit and wait. Visit your kin in the hospital, or something."

"Yeah, sure." Al rose and waved for Fergie to follow. "I'll do just that." He headed out of the room.

As she slid into her side of the front seat, Fergie said, "I'm guessing you have no intention of just waiting on a call from Aaron."

"You'd make money on that bet." He started the truck's engine. "We're back to our one slender thread. We can swing by and round up Tanner so he's not stuck home alone, then we'll see if anything is stirring at Grunderson's place."

Chapter Twenty-two

The sky was fading to darkness when Al pulled his truck into the parking lot at Madrigal Joe's Coffee Shop. Inside, Fred stood behind the counter, looking haggard.

Al bought a couple coffees, which couldn't hurt, considering the evening that lay ahead. As he paid for the coffees he asked, "What happened to Ian Burkov?"

Fred frowned and shook his head. "Just a no-show."

"Ever happen before?"

"Nope. That's why it kind of blindsided me. I had to stay and do the shift myself."

"You call him?"

"Yep. Turns out his phone's been disconnected. Damn shame, too. He was one good counter guy. Dependable, too. Guess I'll have to put up a sign for help wanted. Hey, are you interested, by any chance? An older guy like you might be just what I need."

"Gee, thanks for the compliment. But I'm trying as hard as I can to be retired."

"Well, good luck with that."

?

With less moon shining above and nerves stretched piano-wire tight, Al eased his truck up Grunderson's lane and once again backed into the cozy spot from which they could watch without being seen. He fretted that Grunderson might have taken walks on his property and spotted vehicle tracks going into the woods, but a brief rain and some hearty wind that came with it might have helped obfuscate any trace of Al and Fergie's coming and goings.

"This is the worst part of any case." Al held his binoculars close and stared at the house. "The endless waiting and watching, with no other worthwhile lead."

"Not to mention your idea of the ideal stakeout food."

"What's wrong with coffee, Diet Cokes, and beef jerky?"

"You may have been noticing that I've been slipping my share of the deluxe eats to Tanner."

"Don't give him too much jerky. It may give him gas, and that's the last thing we want inside the truck at this hour."

"We could also try some other ways to track Ian Burkov, our missing night barista."

"We'll see. Clayton passed on that he's missing to our crack FBI contact, Aaron, as well. If anyone can find him, they should be able to. But I have a feeling he's going to be hard to find, disappearing into thin air the way he did."

"Completely off the grid, eh? Whatever was on that card might have spooked him."

"I wish to hell I knew what that was."

"Clayton said that Aaron assured him that the FBI would call you when they knew."

"Yeah, sure. I'll be sitting up and waiting for that."

"That's the thing about this mess, isn't it? People just disappear."

"Yeah. Gerta, then Eliska, now Ian. Poof! But I'll tell you one thing. If I was Grunderson, I'd be doing more about it than he seems to be doing."

"Unless he knows something."

"Which he certainly isn't sharing with us."

The living-room lights were on bright enough that Al could see Grunderson's tall, spare shape rise from a chair and head out of the room, perhaps to the kitchen for a beverage. In a few moments, he lumbered back in and sat. Nothing he did seemed hurried. At nearly midnight, the lights came on in an upstairs bedroom, then the lights downstairs went off. As drama went, it was the flattest show Al had seen in some time. He felt no sense of urgency emanating from the house.

They sat and stared at the lights behind the pulled drapes until, at last, they went out. They waited another hour and a half. Nothing. Al started the truck. Tanner wagged his tail, eager to be heading home. He climbed into Fergie's lap and looked out the windshield at the lines of the road ahead coming their way like a strobe light.

?

Light was barely seeping into the bedroom past the closed blinds when Al woke up. He knew at once something felt very wrong. He sat up, tried to move his right arm, and felt pain shoot outward from deep within his shoulder. With his other hand, he sought to locate the source. The knife of stabbing pain seemed to emanate from deep inside the shoulder joint.

Fergie came out of the bathroom in a robe, her hair twisted up in a towel. She saw him trying to move his arm, attempting to reach up the way he would to comb his hair, then grimacing at the effort. "What's the matter with you?"

"I don't know. Maybe it'll work itself out."

"Did you sleep on it wrong?"

"That's possible, or the pillows are too hard, or I lifted or twisted at something yesterday I can't remember."

"Or your age is catching up with you. It could just be a touch of arthritis or even bursitis."

"It doesn't matter what it is." He heard the edge in his own voice but couldn't help it. "I just need to be fit just now, given what we may run into at any moment."

"Well, what would Batman do?"

"You're not helping."

"Disagree." She rubbed her towel on her still-damp red hair.

He looked around the room and spotted a pair of chrome dumb-bells he was using to prop open the closet door. *Perfect.* He hoisted one carefully with the offending arm and shoulder, bent over, and moved the dumbbell around in a widening circle.

"What are you doing?"

"A gym instructor was helping someone work through a rotator-cuff injury once. This is how you warm up the inside of the shoulder socket." He eased from the swirling to a few curls, taking the weight all the way to his chest.

"Is it working?"

"Only a little." He paused, put the dumbbell down, and tried to reach up as if to comb his hair. Fierce shooting pains stabbed outward from the shoulder's core. "Crap. Crap. Crap. I sure didn't need this just now."

"You're just—"

"Please don't say 'getting older' again."

"Okay. You're a spring chicken. You're a babe. All men fear you. All women want you. You're a..."

He didn't hear the rest. He went inside the bathroom to take a very warm shower and rub at the shoulder. The massage and hot water helped a little, but he feared he was going to have to work on the joint for days instead of minutes. An injury or weakness was the last thing he needed.

?

The second Al and Fergie entered Bonnie's hospital room, Maury looked up from the chair beside the bed and asked, "What's wrong with you? You're tilting, Al."

"It's a hint of his years paying a cameo visit," Fergie said.

Maury, wearing a blue arm sling, held Little Al in a bundle of soft blankets.

Fergie held out her arms and lifted the bundle to her own shoulder. To Bonnie, she said, "You're looking good for someone who has endured a snakebite and a preemie by C-section."

"Yeah. I'm a pip," Bonnie said. "At least I'm ready to get to work. Don't you know, someone from human resources stopped by and offered me my old job back here. Apparently, the hospital administrator, the evil archduchess of health care, Hermina Vanderhausen, put the idea in their ear. They as good as hinted they might do something about my large and growing bill here, too."

"Are you thinking about it?"

"She's practically made up her mind," Maury said. "We're going to have to get out of here soon. At least I am, though I may wait to go with Bonnie and the baby."

"We don't need a higher hospital bill than we already have," Bonnie said.

"I think you should both stay here as long as you can." Al's stare fixed on Maury.

"Why?"

"You're safer here."

"What are you into this time?"

"Nothing just yet. But if we do, it's apt to be on the dangerous side if we get where we need to be."

"And if you don't?"

"Then we've failed."

"Oh." Maury thought for a moment. "We've been so focused on our mess, snakebite, baby, me getting shot and all, that we quite forgot what you're up to. How are you coming along at finding that missing girl?"

"Right in the middle of a hopeless tangle, with hardly a single direction to take. Other than that, fine." Fergie patted the baby's back.

Al stood by the foot of Bonnie's bed, feeling awkward and out of his element. He wanted to rub his sore shoulder but made himself not reach up to it.

A bulky shape filled the doorway. Al's first glance took in the imposing figure of a woman in a taupe business suit with white blouse and a red scarf knotted as a tie. She had an extra chin and a bosom like a battleship, reminding him more than a little of the late Queen Victoria.

"Ahem. I hope I'm not interrupting. I'm Hermina Vanderhausen."

"The hospital administrator," Bonnie said.

Al hoped on hope that Maury's mouth wouldn't open to say, "The Big Kahuna." He could practically see the thought niggling in his brother's mind. It would be so like him.

"My soon-to-be brother-in-law, Al Quinn, and his friend 'Fergie,' Ferguson Jergens," Bonnie said.

The woman extended a hand, which Al shook, then Fergie though she had to reach around the baby.

"Ahem. I see." Ms. Vanderhausen's eyes swept the room. Something seemed to be on her mind. She fixed on Bonnie.

"Let's see, Bonnie here is thirty-seven, if I recall her file correctly, and the offer still stands to have you come back as a nurse." She turned to Maury. "And you're in your sixties, correct?"

"Well, yeah."

"And yet you two managed to have a baby." She stared at Maury. "What did you do, rob a sperm bank?"

Bonnie chuckled, and all heads swung toward her. "He didn't need to. He's their lifelong biggest donor."

That got an arched eyebrow out of Ms. Vanderhausen. She turned back to Maury. "I hear you put rubber stickers on the floor of the shower here. Why?"

"So Bonnie wouldn't fall."

"And you were seen straightening rugs in the hallways near the elevators. Why?"

"Same reason. Someone could have tripped."

"I think you had better come along to my office, Mr. Maurice Quinn. We need to have a chat."

"Uh-oh. In trouble again." Maury shrugged and followed her out of the room.

"Hmm. What do you think is going on there?" Fergie asked Bonnie. "I always heard she was a pretty tough cookie."

"Yeah, she kinda is," Bonnie said. "The staff nickname for her is The Hammer, and it's not because she always goes about spreading sweetness and sunshine. She's the strictest disciplinarian anyone's ever seen."

"Oh dear," Al said. "Maury's not about to get a flogging, is he?"

"I wish I could tell you no," Bonnie said. "Frankly, I wouldn't put it past her."

?

While Al negotiated driving his truck through the stop-and-go nearly parking lot that Austin's traffic became during rush hour, Fergie said, "That lady was kind of scary."

"As much as the Bone Lady?"

"Oh, no way. But I was just fretting over poor Maury."

"Poor Maury has gotten himself into this particular quagmire all on his own."

"So you think having a child, getting shot, and facing the possibility of marriage is a quagmire?"

"I didn't say that. At least I don't think I did. Let's focus on the Bone Lady. We're nearly to her place."

"Way to go. Use the trump card of someone even scarier."

Their slog through traffic meant the Bone Lady was almost certainly home, and that proved to be so. She swung the door open at Al's knock. She wore jeans, a red-and-white-checked shirt with pearl buttons, and oiled Red Wing work boots. She looked around behind them, perhaps checking to see if they had brought Gerta with them.

"Come on in. I just made a pot of coffee." As she handed each of them a mug, she asked, "Anything new?"

Al shook his head. "How about on your end?"

"The FBI has been nosing around."

"That's not a bad thing if they somehow locate Gerta."

"I get the feeling that's about the last thing they care about."

"You might be right. But please wait. Let me keep at this."

"I'm okay with the notion of doing something myself."

"Please wait," Fergie said.

The Bone Lady frowned. "We'll see. We'll just see."

Chapter Twenty-three

Tanner looked out the side window from where he sat on Fergie's lap. He seemed eager, a hound to the chase. Al took his right hand off the steering wheel and reached over to pat him.

"What are you up to here?" Fergie asked.

"Trying to shake things up and try something different, something no one else has tried. Don't forget. You kind of hinted at this before, just not the particular way I'm going to try going about it."

"Okay, I guess. Your track record for getting results from zany approaches is far better than mine."

"What I didn't care for in our stakeout of Grunderson is that he did nothing. He went to the kitchen a time or two, perhaps for a beverage. But he seemed calm. Too calm."

"I guess that's true for someone whose daughter has gone missing. And he hasn't even filed a missing-person report, has he?"

"Nope. Maybe he isn't exactly calm inside, but he's sure as hell not doing much."

"I'd be going crazy, fretting every which way, the way the Bone Lady is doing."

"I think we have to give him a rest for the moment. If he knows something or has a hand he's holding, he isn't apt to share it. He's hardly been the gregarious *bon homme* sort."

"So? We're onward to where?"

"I called Madrigal Joe's Coffee Shop, and hard-working Fred still hasn't heard a word or gotten anything like an explanation from his missing barista, Ian Burkov. I think that's where we have to take our shot in the dark."

"How? Wasn't that pretty much a dead end?"

"I've got something in mind. It may be thin, but it's all we have."

At the apartment complex, Al took a leash out of the glove box and clipped it to Tanner's collar.

"Really, Sherlock?" Fergie's brow furrowed.

"We use what we have."

The door to Ian's apartment was closed, but after only a moment or two of fiddling the lock, Al opened the door.

"Missed your calling in life," Fergie muttered.

Al dropped the leash and let Tanner sniff about. He went over to the closet himself and peered inside. "Aha."

"What'd you find?"

"It's what I didn't find. Do you remember that worthless pair of jeans we saw hanging in the closet the last time?"

"Yeah."

"Well, they're gone."

"And?"

"I had a favorite pair of jeans once. I wore them until they were past even Goodwill wanting them, held together with rough stitches and patches. My mother thought she was doing me a favor and threw them out. Gave me a brand-new pair of shiny blue jeans to replace them. I nearly cried."

"You think he risked coming back to his apartment for those lousy pants?"

"I would have."

Tanner's sniffing had covered the corners and had taken him to the door again. Al went over and picked up the end of the leash.

"What if the trail only leads to where he got into a car and drove away?"

"What if it doesn't?"

"But what if it does?"

"Then we're not any worse off than we were."

Tanner tugged at the leash, a sign he had picked up a scent. Al opened the door to the apartment, and out they shot. Tanner's little legs churned, each leg muscling out straight as he tugged Al along.

Al braced for the inevitable, the dog stopping where the trail disappeared when Ian had climbed into a car. Instead, Tanner continued pulling along the sidewalk that went past the other doors of apartments.

At the end of the row of apartments, Tanner pulled even harder to get Al to come around to the back of the last apartment.

Al turned to Fergie though Tanner strained at his leash. "You'd better stay here by the front door. This may be the place. Give me time to get to the back, and start knocking as loud as you can."

She was tugging her Smith & Wesson out of her ankle holster as Al and Tanner passed around the corner until he could no longer see her. He wished he'd thought to slip his Sig Sauer into the small of his back, but he'd been more surprised than not to have Tanner eagerly pulling him along.

If he'd still been an active member of the sheriff's department and not outside his jurisdiction area anyway, he'd have called for backup about then. That was the nature of being an ad hoc PI. *Well, I'm here now.* The time had come to see if his flickering brainstorm of an idea had any weight to it.

The back porch was similar to all the others, with a white waist-high wooden railing and a couple windows that could look out on the back alley if the blinds weren't pulled. There was little to see. A parking lot stretched up to a couple of green dumpsters on the far side, and half a dozen cars were parked in the lot, with one white pickup on the far side, tucked under the shade of a sprawling mimosa tree. He thought he saw a flicker of something in the truck, then heard Fergie hammering away at the front door.

If he's smart, he'll just stay in there. However, nobody inside would have a way of knowing who was banging away at the other end of the apartment.

He was about to step closer to see if the back door was locked when Tanner growled. A window to his right on the back of the place slid up: first the screen, then the glass. A large sneaker at the end of faded jeans started out the window.

Al crouched low and pressed closer to the back of the place so that he couldn't be seen at first glance. He held Tanner's mouth shut to keep him from barking though he pulled and lunged, trying to get at the scent he'd been following. That had to be Ian.

"Wait. Wait!" someone said from inside.

Ian clambered all the way out and stood looking left and right.

Al leaned out to see if Ian held a gun. He didn't.

Ian spotted Al at almost the same time a man's head stuck out the back window. "Get back inside!"

A shot sounded. The bullet hit Ian in the shoulder, knocking him back into the brick of the apartment's outer wall.

"No. No. Nyet!" the man in the window yelled.

Another shot sent him flying backward and out of sight.

Al crouched as low as he could get to the ground, covering Tanner with his own body. He knew guns. That didn't sound like a hunting rifle. It sounded like an AR-15.

Ian tried to stand, perhaps to make a run for it. A bullet slammed into his chest, pounding him back into the bricks again. He fell in a slump to the ground.

The shooting stopped, and the white truck across the way peeled out in a spray of gravel, too far away for Al to catch even a glimpse of the plates.

Fergie came running around the side of the building, her gun up and ready to fire, though a snub-nose pistol was a far cry from what could have done any good, given the range. "Are you okay?"

Al stood from where he'd been feeling for a pulse at Ian's throat and not getting one. He eased up to the window and looked inside. "I am, but I can't say the same for these two."

He had to pull at Tanner to keep him away from the corpse. "You're former city police. Maybe you should make the call."

"I don't know if I need to."

Al could hear two sirens, each approaching from a different direction. "Yep. Sounds like someone already did."

Chapter Twenty-four

Al put Tanner in his truck, petted him on the head, cracked the windows, and closed the door on him. He headed back to the bright lights, where a crime-scene crew was putting the two victims in body bags.

Once back in the bright lights and blinking, he eased down onto a patch of grass where Fergie waited. He reached out to take her hand.

A tall fellow in a brown suit stood from where he'd been crouched by one corpse. He came toward them, frowning and rubbing at the stubble on his long chin.

Al had already been introduced in the growing darkness outside the apartment building to Lt. J. D. Strummers, Fergie's former boss. The demeanor of her whispered aside to Al let him know that, like Sheriff Clayton, he was a boss with whom she hadn't joshed about often. He gave them both a curt handshake and a couple of notepads to scratch out their statements.

"Be as detailed as possible," he said, using the most words Al had heard from him. The lieutenant knew they were both former law enforcement and he couldn't charge them with anything, but he'd been brusque, adding to the tension of an already-gritty moment.

When Strummers had lumbered all the way to them, Fergie looked up and said, "I thought you were with organized crime now."

"I am." He had the long pockmarked face of someone who had fought a rough bout with acne as an adolescent and lost.

"Oh. And these guys are...?"

"All I know about these particular guys is that they're both some kind of Russian immigrants. Dead ones now. But someone didn't bother to gun them down just because they were immigrants. They must have been up to something. Do you know anything about that?"

"You find anything inside the apartment?"

"Of course not."

He crouched down until his face was near theirs. He peered at them closely, not expecting anything but taking a quick inventory. "You have to ask yourself what I'm asking myself just now."

Al said nothing and figured Fergie gave the man her expectant raised eyebrow.

"You two are of no particular significance to me or my department." He paused. "I don't say that to be cruel but just to state the facts. And these two victims are low-level nobodies. Foot soldiers. Russians, but otherwise uninteresting. So why was someone of my rank called out at this hour to look into this? And why did I get calls from both the county sheriff and the FBI's agent in residence?"

Al shrugged. He felt Fergie's hand tighten on his.

The lieutenant peered into their faces, still not finding what he sought. "Someone felt something needed cleaning or covering up. In taking the risk to do that, they have only sent up a brighter blue flare. Do you get me? Whatever they got close to was poison, and it bit them."

He stared at Fergie. "Don't let whatever is behind this bite you."

?

Fergie climbed into bed right after Al fed Tanner. He was brushing his teeth with his left hand to avoid aggravating his right shoulder when his cell phone rang. Of course it was Clayton.

"I just took a call, at home, at this hour, from an annoyed federal agent who feels you're not playing ball."

"I hope you told him where to stick his plaything."

"Al. Come on, now. Work with me."

"I'll work with *you*. But I have yet to receive anything from that fellow."

"I read copies of the statements you and Fergie made to the city police. You're sticking to your story of following a hunch?"

"Yeah, one that was far too flimsy to share. I had to bring my own dog in on the case, and the odds were against getting as far as we did."

"Yet you succeeded, to a degree. What that lead got you was two dead men with no hope of finding with whom they work."

"I'm usually not prone to guessing, but in this case I'm prone to agree with Lieutenant Strummers that their employer was the one who decided to cancel their stamps. Whether that's an individual or an organization, I can't tell. I'm no closer to solving what I'm working on, which is a missing girl. Someone just muddied that trail and wiped out my only fragile lead."

"Seems someone is going to a great deal of bother to ensure that there is no trail."

"Trail or no trail, I still have to find a girl, one who is probably scared and about to give up hope."

"Good luck with that. Just remember to play well with others."

"To that end, where is Agent Aaron staying? He knows where to find me, but I don't know where to reach him."

"He's camped at one of those residence-inn sort of places out closer to Lake Travis, not all that far from where you live."

"Do you think that's near where he expects to uncover anything?"

"I have no idea what he thinks."

"Ah. So he shares about as much with you as he does with me."

?

Sometimes lights came on. Just as often, they went off until everything was black. But the air was always dank and the bars cold.

Men moved about in the distance, clanking and banging about in their clumsy way. They only came closer when it was time to take away the other girls. The two of them were left behind. They didn't know why.

In one of the dark stretches, they huddled close and hugged each other.

"I've never been so scared in my life."

"Someone will come."

"How do you know?"

"Because that's all I have left inside me, knowing that."

Chapter Twenty-five

"I remember this place," Fergie said. "Wasn't it part of an upscale chain that didn't get its demographic market research right?"

Al saw the inn he was after just ahead. "Something like that. It was supposed to be used for retreats, group getaways, and such. But it wasn't right on the water, and it was just far enough out of the heart of town to be more of a bother than a blessing. The chain sold it, and the Golden Eagle Skyway Retreat began its less-glorious existence. Not too high-priced, not too low."

"About right for a government employee on a per diem?"

"It's where Clayton hinted he could be found."

Al pulled his truck into the lot. On the far side, not too far from the lobby, three black SUVs were parked in a snug row.

"Do you think this is a good idea?"

"No."

"But you're going to do it anyway."

"Looks that way."

He eased the truck into a space at the far end of the lot, backing in-to the shade of a sycamore tree on the landscaped grounds. Everything looked as green as a golf course, so the sprinklers probably ran every night.

Al got his binoculars out of the glove box and handed the smaller Nikon pair to Fergie.

"So we just wait?"

"We wait."

Al couldn't remember when he'd ever spent so much time on stake-outs. They weren't always the answer and only sometimes added a glim-mer that led to something bigger. Sometimes, they led nowhere at all.

That had been pretty much their experience in the case so far. They were a hard way to spend time, but they were all Al had at the moment, reaching and grasping but getting little or nothing. He hoped those Bu folks were being more productive with their time. He blinked and lifted his binoculars again.

After a stark half hour of nothing going on whatsoever, Fergie lowered her glasses and slid closer. She reached over and started to knead the muscles of his right shoulder.

"Do you mind?"

"No. It feels good. Don't ever get old, Fergie."

"You know we're the exact same age." Fergie pressed harder and got a moan out of him. "I wish we'd had time to swing by and check on Bonnie and Maury at the hospital."

"They'll be safer there than anywhere else just now."

"I guess I would have liked another peek at Little Al, too."

"We'll have the pitter-patter of his feet around soon enough when we're all back at the house."

"Is that how you pictured things for your retirement years?"

"Not in my wackiest dreams."

"I can't say this is how I envisioned things either, but—"

"Hold that thought, Fergie. He just stepped outside, and he's by himself. He's looking left and right, even in this direction, but we're too far away, and light is failing."

Fergie had her glasses up. "I see him. He's climbing into one of the Bu wagons."

Al started the truck's engine.

"Remember to hold back."

"Really? I thought I might just hook up to his back end and let him tow us."

"I know you have a lot of tailing experience, some of it from high school."

"That would be Maury."

"But this guy's probably better than most at spotting a tail."

Al hung back as much as he dared, but Aaron wasn't afraid to step on the gas. When Al had to flip on his lights, he knew it would be harder to stay unnoticed since traffic was thinning out as they traveled on the two-lane back roads.

Fifteen minutes into the exercise, Al came around a bend and saw the black SUV pulled over to the right beside the road in a gravel patch that allowed the daily mail carrier to swing in to the mailbox of a house that was out of sight back down a long lane.

Al kept going, hoping Aaron was just on the cell phone or something. After a mile or so, he pulled over himself. In just a few ticks, the black SUV came down the road and pulled over until its front bumper nearly touched Al's truck.

Aaron climbed out of the driver's side and walked up to the truck. Al rolled his window down and waited.

"What the devil do you think you're on about?" Aaron wore a dark-blue windbreaker that probably concealed a shoulder holster.

Al always thought the use of a ticked-off British accent was more lame than imposing.

"Just out having an evening drive," Al said.

Aaron leaned forward until his forearms rested on Al's truck. That let his jacket hang open so Al could see that he indeed wore a DeSantis holster. Al didn't have to look closer to know the weapon was probably a Glock 22, chock full of the Bu standard .40-caliber ammo. The gesture was cheap, like a minor hoodlum letting Al see his piece peeking out of his belt to make him seem more dangerous.

"Knock it off. You get in my way, and I'll see you're charged with interfering with an investigation."

"How can I be interfering when we're supposed to be working together? Do you have any other leads I should know about?"

Aaron started to open his mouth but closed it and probably spent the time counting to ten in his mind. "Just knock it off. Okay?" He spun on his heel and walked back to his vehicle.

Al didn't wait on him. He pulled out onto the road and kept going and didn't see the SUV following.

"So that's it? You're not going to tail him anymore?"

"It wasn't about the tail, anyway. It was to see what irritates him."

"I don't know him all that well, but I'd guess just about everything does."

Chapter Twenty-six

"If I had a nickel for every time I wished I had a nickel for that, we'd be up to our ear bones in nickelodeon music," Al said.

"Hmpf. I just said I wished we were almost anywhere else in all of Texas other than sitting here like two lumps on a log." Fergie dug deeper into the muscles of Al's shoulder.

Al winced when she pressed against a nerve, but he said, "Don't stop." He held the binoculars up with his left hand and kept them fixed on the lights in Grunderson's windows.

"Why doesn't he seem more worried?"

"Maybe he is but just doesn't show it."

"Well, at the very least, he's moving about in a more animated way this evening. None of those leisurely strolls to the kitchen or bathroom and back. He's darn near bustling about. Maybe he's going to go out."

"I hope so. I'd be glad to move. Not that I don't enjoy the night sounds of crickets and frogs."

Al had backed his truck once again into the snug copse of sumac and cedar. He could barely see through to the house, and that view was sometimes blocked as the breeze swayed a limb across the narrow gap. He was certain they couldn't be seen from the house, especially as dark as the evening was and with lights on inside the house.

Tanner stirred restlessly behind them in the truck's extended cab. He'd tried a few times to move forward and climb into a lap, but Al had pushed him back. With Maury and Bonnie still both in the hospital, he hated to leave the dog at home.

Fergie paused her massaging of Al's shoulder to pick up her binoculars. "He sure is moving about more. This is the most animated we've seen him."

As if on cue, most of the lights in the house clicked off. Grunderson stepped out his front door, barely visible in the shadows and dim light of a sliver of a moon.

He climbed into his car, which sat just outside the garage door, started the engine, and flipped on his lights.

Al's insides fluttered with the thrill of something about to happen. After all the waiting while expecting very little, hanging back and tailing a car felt good. Of course, he might expect a letdown if Grunderson was merely headed to get coffee or go to the grocery. So late at night, though, Al dared hope for something greater.

"Does this feel just a little too easy to you?"

"Maybe. But if this leads to Gerta, I'm willing to grab at it and welcome an easier solution than expected. We've been bouncing around too long and getting too little. A lucky break will be fine with me."

A couple of times, Grunderson seemed to slow down, so Al had to slow down as well. Once, he turned off the road into a lane and waited a few ticks before easing out to follow again. The last thing Al wanted to do was spook him.

As they drifted farther from the bigger roads and the lights of clusters of dwellings, Al's hopes grew. They were in the sort of middle of nowhere he had hoped for.

Al, who had driven through nearly every part of the county during his years on the sheriff's department, recognized where they were heading. They had cleaned out a number of meth labs out that way some years before.

He drove past a wrecking yard where, over the top of a fence, he could see an ocean of crashed vehicles of every shape and size. Next came a scrapyard, then a cement plant, and finally a row of warehouses too run-down to be of any use. He'd been expecting to find them knocked down and something useful taking their place—no such luck, so far. They stood like the wrecked ships around Pearl Harbor, but with a far less patriotic message.

Grunderson turned in way down the row ahead. Al hung back. The final warehouse in the row would be there. Abandoned train tracks crossed the road not long after that.

Much of Travis County was under massive development—houses, businesses, and growth of all kinds—but not out there. The remoteness encouraged Al.

He didn't recall another way out from around the back, so he gave Grunderson a few moments to get settled. He eased his truck closer, headlights off, and parked before going around the corner. Al turned off the dome lights before he and Fergie got out. She had her ankle holster and her Glock 19.

Al took his Sig Sauer out of the glove box and slipped it inside his belt at the small of his back. Putting it there made him think twice. The twinge of pain it took to get it out might slow him, but he was too late in life to suddenly switch to being a lefty. They were as ready as they could be.

Tanner moved to the front seat to follow them.

Al had cracked the windows. He held up a hand. "Stay!"

At least Tanner didn't whine or bark as they moved away from the truck.

The wind picked up and snapped at Al's hair. Fergie's long red hair swung out to one side, and the dim light of the slim moon and stars made her look like an intense addition to ZZ Top's band.

Al led the way along the front of the warehouse and was first to stick his head around the corner. Nothing. No car. No Grunderson. *Where in the devil could he have gone?*

Fergie took a peek then eased back to whisper, "Something's not right."

Al agreed with that. He eased all the way around the corner and slid along the weathered siding of the warehouse, touching it with one hand as he moved forward. The texture of the building was coarse, as though the wind had sanded away at it for years.

At last, he came to a row of loading docks. Grunderson's BMW was tucked tightly between two of them where it couldn't be seen until they were almost on it—but no Grunderson.

Al clambered up onto the dock and held out his left hand to give Fergie a boost to join him.

The double-wide doors at the back of the dock were slightly ajar. Al pushed one side open with a slow haunted-house creak until it was wide enough to step through. Under his breath, he cursed the noise, but he could do little about it. At least he got no response from within the cavernous building.

Even without a hand light, he could sense the insides stood empty. He couldn't see the barest hint of where Grunderson had gone.

"I think this calls for a bloodhound," he whispered to Fergie.

Back at the truck, he hooked up Tanner to his leash, petted him on the head, and got a small penlight from the glove box. He and Fergie headed back to their open doorway. All of Al's confidence about wrapping this up swiftly and easily was seeping like sand out of his boot toes. A glance at Fergie's face confirmed she was sharing some of the same eerie apprehension the empty warehouse conveyed.

Al gave Tanner a chance to pick up a scent by Grunderson's BMW then hung on while Tanner headed off in a direction Al wouldn't have taken first.

The wind blew in a scraping rasp against the sides of the warehouse's empty shell. Somewhere, a wooden window or shutter was banging repeatedly as the breeze swung it open and closed, again and again. *Bam. Bam. Bam.*

Tanner tugged in a straight line, finally halting at a wide closed door at the back of the warehouse. He fixed on it, so Al aimed the narrowed beam of his penlight on the floor. By bending forward and moving Tanner to one side, he could make out a line. He followed it until he could make out another seam joining at a right angle. The dust had been swept away in the area.

"It's some kind of doorway that opens to a lower place," Fergie whispered.

Al nodded, not that she could hear it.

He swung the beam of light along the inside of the back wall then moved close to her ear. "There's another one of these over there, and it looks like it's open," he whispered.

Tanner tugged that way.

As they got closer to the gaping gateway to below, Al could see the faintest glimmer of light coming from the opening. Basements were not common in Texas. He'd only seen a few. They usually had a special purpose, like storing something that needed to stay cool or keeping data files safe or growing mushrooms, for all Al knew.

At the top of the ramp, they paused. Fergie's hand reached out to clamp on his arm. Tanner gave a low growl.

"Shhh!" He bent to pat Tanner's head. Then he started down the ramp, Fergie still hanging onto his arm.

The area below didn't seem nearly as big as the warehouse above, but Al could make out a row of vehicles parked along one side. Around the bend of a partition, he located what was probably the source of the dim light.

He and Fergie moved in careful steps in that direction, although Tanner tugged harder as they progressed first around a corner and then into another open room. At the far right of that room, Al could make out three iron-bar cages, the sort lions are kept in at a circus or zoo. In the nearest one weren't any beasts, just two frightened girls.

Fergie started to rush forward, but Al reached out to slow her. He looked around but didn't see anyone.

As they got closer, Al could make out Eliska's pale round face. The girl clinging to her was Gerta. She had the high cheekbones and coppery cast of her mother's face, but with a youthful tautness and none of the crow's feet at the corners of her eyes.

Most of all, Al wondered where Grunderson was. He'd entered the warehouse first.

Fergie shot across in a burst to the cage. She rattled at its door, but it seemed locked tight.

Al looked around, flashing his penlight beam wherever he thought someone might hang a key. Nobody had left a ring of keys hanging nearby, like at the jail in Andy Griffin's Mayberry.

Tanner began a low growl that turned louder.

The hair stood up on the back of Al's neck. He started to reach toward the small of his back.

"I wouldn't do that if I were you." The deep voice behind him had a trace of accent, Russian perhaps—at the very least, Eastern European.

The two girls were holding their mouths and pointing.

Fergie turned around, and her shoulders sagged.

Al dared a look behind in the direction Tanner had turned to growl even more loudly while tugging at his leash.

Five men stood in a row, four holding weapons. Al saw two AK-47s, a MAC-10, and an AR-15, and the last man, almost twice as big as the others, had just his ham-sized fists clenched at his sides. Two tears tattooed just below the corner of his left eye did little to comfort Al. Those indicated he'd killed two men and was proud of it. All five had the kind of faces that might have never smiled in their lives. They all looked to have slightly different ethnic backgrounds as well, matching the diversity of their choice of weapons. In the distant shadowy background, Al could make out the sounds and occasional glimpse of others moving about. From the backlight, he could see the shapes of men carrying what could be cases of weapons or small coffins. He guessed that anywhere from twenty to fifty people were working away down there.

I sure walked into it this time.

"You with the dog, toss your piece to the floor. This way."

Al held out a hand for Fergie to take. He calculated what damage he could do if he charged the men. At the end of his calculation, he did as he was told, hoping for a better opportunity. He watched as the big man, whom one of them had just called Stomper, went over to pat down Fergie and found her ankle gun as well as her Glock.

Tanner growled.

"Someone had better hang onto that leash, or you're going to have the deadest dog in a three-county area." That voice was different from the first Al had heard, which didn't make him feel any better.

The men came closer, herding them toward the middle cage of the three. Its door stood open. Al felt as low and miserable as he ever had in his life, more about Fergie and Tanner than himself—that and he had failed miserably at rescuing the Bone Lady's daughter.

Al went up on the balls of his feet. He was half a second from trying something, almost anything, when Stomper moved more quickly than expected to tuck his left arm inside Al's right shoulder. He lifted his enormous arm in a come-along hold that had Al on his tiptoes and about to scream as loudly as he ever had in his life. He held it back, in spite of a fire of pain that felt as if the arm had been just about ripped off.

Pushed inside the cage, Al had broken out in a sweat from the throbbing pain in his shoulder. He realized that he was taking big gulps of air and that Fergie knew why he was panting. His face must have been flushed a lively pink hue.

The steel gate clanged shut behind them. Al felt at the bars—solid steel. He wondered how the hell the cages came to be there but fussed more with himself at being in one of them. He let go of the leash for the first time. Tanner rushed at the bars, but they were too close together for him to get through. Al stepped close to Fergie and put his arms around her. "I'm sorry."

Over her shoulder, he saw two other figures emerge from the shadows. They came toward the cages.

One was Grunderson. He avoided looking toward Al and Fergie, his eyes fixed on the girls.

The man with him had close-set eyes and black growth on his face that was longer than his buzz-cut hair. He wore U.S. military camo fatigues. Al doubted very much that the man had ever served in any branch of American military, but he had the bearing and scowl of a military lifer.

Stomper went to the cage that held the two girls, took a key out of his pocket, and unlocked the gate. The two girls shot out of the cage, and Eliska rushed to hug her father. Gerta just stood close, looking forlornly toward Fergie, Al, and Tanner.

"That son of a bitch sold us out. He traded us for his daughter," Fergie muttered.

"I fear you're right. But there's not a helluva lot we can do about that just now." Al continued to feel around at the gate and bars of their cage, but he couldn't find any weakness.

As Grunderson walked past them with the two girls, he wouldn't look at them.

"Turn around, damn you," Al said. "Look at us. See where you've left us."

Grunderson lowered his head and muttered, "I don't want to see these people or know who they are."

"Just make sure Gerta gets back to her mother," Al called after him.

Grunderson didn't look back, but Gerta did.

Chapter Twenty-seven

Fergie's fingers gripped and felt the harsh reality of the cold steel of the unbendable bars. Men moved about in the dimly lit distance, some occasionally visible, most not. She and Al had not talked all that much about their pasts, especially about Al's ex-wife, Abbie, and what had happened between her and Maury.

For her own part, she had never brought up what she thought of as her "champagne years" and the men she had dated twenty to thirty years before, usually a few years older than herself, who had plied her with Mumm, Piper, Bollinger, Cristal, and even Dom Perignon. She'd picked at her salmon or ruby trout at some of the better restaurants and had had the occasional crème brûlée, but none of that had made her feel nearly as alive as her last year or two with Al. She had never shared how she felt about that and wasn't sure if she was ready or able to do so now.

?

Al sat down on the hard metal floor of the cage, and Fergie eased down beside him. He put one arm around her shoulders and pulled Tanner closer with the other. The three of them huddled close.

"I'm really sorry," Al said, "to you both."

"Oh, Al." Fergie rubbed at his right shoulder. "How's that feel? Any better?"

"You know, I think that lug Stomper actually did my shoulder some good by wrenching me around like a soft pretzel the way he did. Now that the massive amount of pain is going away, I'm starting to feel all right. Maybe a nerve was pinched and he freed it."

"Or he dislocated the shoulder, separating the nerve from the area entirely."

"At any rate, I feel much better, like I could do someone some harm now. I'd like to have another shot at that Stomper."

"Oh, Al. He was huge. You'd probably end up giving him your truck keys."

"Speaking of keys, he's the holder of the only way out of this cage."

Fergie sighed. Tanner licked the back of Al's hand.

Only a dim light came from around the distant corner where the men had disappeared. Al could hear sounds that, to his ear, seemed to indicate the group was gathering up the last of their stuff from the warehouse. He guessed they were going to leave the cages. They probably had several other sites like that one. Given the nature of their business, they probably had to move about a good deal.

"Al, what do you think...?"

"I don't think anything just yet. I have a ton of questions but no answers. I'm not even sure I want the answers at the moment."

"Maybe I can answer some of them." The disembodied voice came from the shadows.

A man stepped out of the darkness into the half-light until Al could make out the features of Aaron Masterson. He wondered for a second or two how long the man had been standing in the dark, watching them.

Al stood up and reached to tug Fergie up beside him.

"Get us out of here!" Fergie used a stage whisper.

Aaron chuckled. "I don't think you grasp the big picture of what's going on here." He got close enough to tap at the steel bars of their cage with a knuckle. "I was told these were used to hold the big cats in a circus. Even the great apes couldn't bend the bars and get away."

"You're not going to help us?" Fergie spoke in full voice.

For the briefest time, Al's hopes of surviving had soared, but they suddenly went into a tailspin. "You sack of crap. You've sold out, haven't you?"

"Let's focus for a second on how much of a better detective I am than either of you. You were still thrashing around while I got all the way to these guys. It's comic. Really, it is."

"In time to make a deal with them, apparently," Al said.

"Why didn't they just kill us?" Fergie asked.

"Because I convinced them you guys were leverage in case they needed it—for a brief while, until the move is done. The girls, they were just merchandise. But you two have friends. Clayton, for instance, who might pause if your lives were threatened."

"And if we're dead?" Al said.

"As you will be, after the fire. Then he'll mourn you and bury you with honor, once he sorts out the identities of the charred remains. And he'll wonder for years who did this dastardly thing." Aaron chuckled again. He was having one swell time.

Al looked about. He couldn't see anyone in the shadows surrounding them. He tried not to think of the reality of their situation. *Hold out for the slightest ray of hope.* He knew all too well when he was shucking himself—shucking himself hard just to keep from screaming in rage.

"Who are these men?" Al asked.

He figured it best to keep Aaron talking. He clearly savored having the upper hand. Most FBI agents talked about as much as a statue in the park, but Aaron leaned to the chatty side.

Aaron laughed out loud. "You're going to get a kick out of this. Uncle Sergei, who they call The Brain, is the head of this ragtag bunch. They're not from one background or ethnicity, just a hodgepodge of skilled talent assembled for a sole purpose. They call themselves Nechelovecheskiye, 'the nobodies.' But they are certainly becoming somebodies to their competition, the out-and-out Russian groups, the Armenians, the rest of the up-and-coming lot that even have the Mexican cartels nervous. And why? Because they'll do *anything,* traffic anything, steal anything, and exploit anyone, however young. The lives of people mean very little to them. They're far less family-centric than the Italians, the Russians, or the Mexicans. They can give up a couple of chicks just like that because they can round up thirty more by noon. There're millions, even billions in their operation. As you can guess, with that kind of big money at stake, secrecy is vital."

"Enough to kill off men and buy off federal agents?" Al kept looking for any movement in the shadows. He saw nothing. "How much are you getting out of this?"

"More than you can ever imagine."

"You'd side with them after they killed your leads up the child-porn ladder?"

"These guys didn't do all of that. We discussed it, and I have no reason not to believe them. They'd brag if they had done it. But there isn't a thirty-ought-six rifle among them. Now Trick Gibson, a pro job like that, twenty-two bullets to the eyes? Sure, they did that, and the Minskys as well. Efficient, and it sends a certain message about trying to see too much. The guy you have to worry about is Stomper, who would far prefer using his fists over any knife. Even though I've barely been with these guys, I've already gotten to see him get nasty with those big boots of his. Nasty. Bad-dreams-for-weeks nasty."

What bothered Al the most was the smug satisfaction, even arrogance, in Aaron's voice. He had information that could have solved at least Gibson's and the Minskys' murders, and he'd done nothing about it. He'd sold out on everything he was supposed to believe and serve, and he was damned proud of it.

"How'd you end up selling yourself out to these guys when you could have gone with any of the others, the purer Russian mafia groups or the Mexicans?" Al knew as he spoke that he expected to die along with Fergie and Tanner. Aaron was letting them know far, far too much.

"Because here's where I had the opportunity. Those other groups wouldn't have embraced me because I wasn't one of them. Tight family-like units they are. These guys didn't care about that as long as they could use me. And let me tell you, because of the assembled sort of group they are, these guys are *far* more ruthless, more daring, more willing to take risks as well as take lives. And the money was *so* damn good."

"They listen to you?" Fergie asked.

"Uncle Sergei and his boys, for instance, were split on what to do with you. Most just wanted to snuff you out like cigarette butts. I suggested that keeping you alive for a short spell would give them leverage if they need it. Some want to set fire to the place. It's dry as a tinder box, old wooden building like this. Sergei liked the idea of you all starving until you had to resort to eating the dog or each other. You don't by any chance have any cannibalistic leanings, do you, Fergie?"

"I've got secrets, but that's not one of them."

"And, by the by, the Bu, as well as Clayton, still think I'm in deep undercover."

"You must have something pretty nasty on Grunderson so that he'll stay well-corked and won't call for help. I suppose your pals will be moved out anyway by the time anyone arrives."

"To find what's left of you. You might start practicing that old gladiator gag, the one that goes, 'We who are about to die salute you.'"

Al shrugged.

"You won't be so cavalier in a while. Uncle Sergei promised you to Stomper as a sort of treat, you know, to kill you just before they leave. You've seen the man. You know what sort of thing he might enjoy." He spun and started to walk away.

"How do you stand yourself?" Fergie asked. "The stink of all you are is... has to be despicable even to the woman who gave birth to you."

Aaron paused and looked back. Whatever he was going to say next was cut short by the sound of gunfire.

"Well, crap," he said, yanking his Glock from his shoulder holster. "It's probably those damned Armenians."

Aaron took off at a run.

Al could hear what sounded like shooting back and forth, but he could see nothing. After a few moments of waiting and being able to do nothing, though, he could smell something. *Smoke.* The place was on fire.

Chapter Twenty-eight

For the better part of the next forty minutes, Al and Fergie huddled low on the floor of their cage, hugging each other and Tanner. The fire grew hotter and the flames closer. The shooting increased in waves of intensity.

The worst part was being able to do nothing. Al had tested all the bars and found none of them loose or weak. They needed the key to the lock.

Al knew the sounds of a SWAT or law-enforcement assault team, and that's not what he was hearing. Random shots, a few in singles but most in bursts of automatic fire, came from all directions. It sounded like two hostile factions who didn't care much for each other and were willing to exchange bullets over the notion.

The smoke got thicker by the moment. Fergie began to cough.

Al was, oddly enough, dwelling on all the things that had been bugging him in his life. People were moving closer to his house, crowding him. Maury and Bonnie were running up enormous medical bills and would soon be coming back into his house with a crying baby. Big pharma was ripping off Americans with their jacked-up high prices. All of that seemed to matter a whole helluva lot less just then.

He choked and found it very hard to breathe at all. Tanner was panting. Fergie tried to hold the dog close. She reached out and clutched Al closer, too.

The increasingly dense layer of smoke seemed likely to asphyxiate them before the burning warehouse had a chance to fall on them. Al blinked his eyes and then opened them wider.

Through the smoke and now flames he could see Stomper coming toward them. He seemed to be smiling, if that was even possible for a murderous hulk like him. His expression was not truly human but that of an animal, one that had just gotten out of its cage and was intent on making a kill.

A bare three feet from them, he suddenly stiffened and stood up straighter. His eyes bulged, and he turned his head, trying to look behind himself.

He slowly toppled forward, splitting the smoke and falling in an enormous thud. As soon as he was down, Al could see the Bone Lady, where she had been standing behind him. She held a bloody fixed-blade knife, one with a nine-inch curved blade, just like the one he'd seen in her hand at the butcher's shop.

She bent over the hulk of Stomper's body to fumble in a front pocket and came up with a key. She wiped the blade of the knife on a clean stretch of the back of Stomper's shirt then hurried over to the cage and put the key in. In seconds, she swung the door open.

"How did you...?" Al started to ask.

"The key? He said I could have it."

"How'd you know where to look, that he had it?"

"Gerta. Look, we can have a cozy chat later. Did y'know this place is on fire?"

She ducked low, staying as much as possible beneath the smoke layer, where the air was only slightly fresher. Al held Tanner's leash and Fergie's hand as they followed closely behind her. She seemed to know the best way out, and a body lying here and there along the way might have been part of her source of information. Al didn't look closely to see if they'd been shot or stabbed. He felt it best if he didn't know.

"This way," she hissed.

She bent to move a fallen man from in front of a door. Inside the door, a stairwell of two short flights of cement steps led up to the ground level.

The Bone Lady bent out to peer in both directions. She waved them to follow and broke into a run. Neither Al nor Fergie had a gun. Apparently, neither did the Bone Lady though that hadn't slowed her.

Several vehicles outside were already pulling away from the warehouse, from which huge black clouds of smoke poured. Al could see low flames growing higher along the near side of the building. He heard only a sporadic shot or two.

She led them to an olive-green Jeep Cherokee pulled up close to a chain-link fence.

Al could hear the first of the fire trucks approaching in the distance. He looked back toward the warehouse and didn't see a single vehicle near it. The fire had sent everyone scattering.

"Where's my truck?" Al asked, looking around.

"I had Gerta drive it already to your place."

"Didn't she need a key?"

"Need a key? You're funny," the Bone Lady said. She climbed into the driver's seat. Al and Tanner clambered into the backseat while Fergie rode up front.

"Why'd you do it?" Fergie asked as the Bone Lady shifted gears and took off in a small spray of gravel.

The vehicle slid sideways for a few feet as she worked it up onto the road then pressed down hard enough on the gas to jerk their heads back.

"You got Gerta free from those men. I owed you."

"I hope you haven't tangled yourself in something that will put you and Gerta at risk."

"We were already at risk. But think of it this way. The ones on the other side, they're at risk too, now."

"I suspect they'll nevertheless come after us," Fergie said.

"Not you guys." The Bone Lady turned off onto a road that would take them back to Al's place, but by the long way. A hook-and-ladder fire truck roared by on the road behind them, its siren wailing. Two other department vehicles followed closely after it.

"Why so?" Fergie asked.

The Bone Lady turned to look right at her. "Because for all those dinkheads know, you guys are dead."

"In that case," Al said, "maybe you should swing us past the airport. I know one or two rent-a-wreck agencies where I can get a rental for a cash deposit. We're going to have to stay off the grid for a while."

"Is it the feds you fear?" Fergie asked.

"At this stage, I fear everyone," Al said.

Chapter Twenty-nine

Maury was carrying the baby with his free arm. The other arm was in a blue sling. Fergie had an arm around Bonnie as they slipped out the side door of the hospital at the far end of the parking lot. Tanner's head stuck up inside the rental car's cracked window, his tail wagging as Al led the way to a rust-colored Olds Cutlass parked all the way across the lot.

"What happened to your truck?" Maury asked.

"Long story. We'll have lots of time to share it in a few moments when we're rolling."

"They probably wouldn't have let me check out so early, and with a baby, but me being a nurse and one likely to be working there again soon, here we are." Bonnie puffed as she walked and kept glancing around the parking lot. "What is it we're watching for?"

"Just keep moving," Fergie whispered.

When Al had burst into their room and said they had to "go, go, go and right now," Bonnie had slid out of bed, and Maury hadn't asked a single question. They'd been around Al long enough to feel the raw urgency emanating from him. He winked at them, trying to take the edge off, but he'd helped them gather their things and check out as quickly as possible.

As soon as Bonnie eased into the back seat beside Fergie and Tanner, Maury handed in the baby. "There'll be time to get a car seat later. Hang on tight to Little Al for now."

Al had the car running. Fergie reached over across the back of his seat to rub at his right shoulder. "Are you really better?"

He rolled his shoulder and felt a slight resistance like crumpled paper. The area retained a general ache, but even that was lessening. He felt none of the earlier deep stabs of pain. The shoulder called less attention to itself, which was good since he might just need it.

"Yeah, that guy ought to be a chiropractor."

"He'd be a dead one."

Al pulled away as soon as Maury was inside and clicked his seat belt. He took an exit from the hospital lot different from the one where Maury had gotten shot. He doubted anyone would be waiting there, but he prided himself on learning from experience.

He'd gone barely two blocks when a cruiser pulled out and came up quickly behind him. Al could hear the roar of the Crown Vic's Interceptor motor. The lights on its roof bar flashed red and blue.

"How fast were you going, Al?" Maury asked.

"Within the speed limit, even the hospital's stingy one."

Al pulled over and was fishing for his wallet to get out his license when the driver got out of the sheriff's department cruiser, a big fellow, big enough to be the sheriff himself.

Maury was looking back. "That's Sheriff Clayton, isn't it?"

"Wonder what he wants," Fergie said.

"Guess I'll find out." Al got out of the rental and went back to meet Clayton halfway between the vehicles.

The wind was blowing and tugged at Al's hair. He looked inside the cruiser. *No one else there.* So Clayton was on his own. *Hmm.*

"Where are you headed to?" Clayton said.

"I don't know yet."

"There's someone else at your house."

"I know. I put them there, to be safer than they would be at their own home."

"Mind bringing me up to speed?"

"Well, for one, I'm dead. So are Fergie and Tanner."

"That big warehouse fire?"

"Yep. We were locked in a cage, supposed to die there or be killed."

"I know about the fire. That's not a very clear picture for us so far. How were you involved?"

"Have you ever heard of the Nechelovecheskiye, the Nobodies?"

Clayton reached up to raise the front brim of his hat with an extended finger. His eyes opened wider. "You are keeping high-tone company, aren't you?"

"They're nobody I'd welcome seeing again soon. You can't let anyone know I'm still alive. I mean *anyone.*"

"You have any particular anyone in mind?"

"Look, I'll be happy to explain everything I know or think I know. We've got to get somewhere safe without anyone knowing."

"As it happens, I have such a place," Clayton said. "Follow me, and stay close."

He headed back, got into the cruiser, and turned off the lights. When he pulled out and around, Al eased from the curb and followed.

"Where are we going?" Fergie asked.

"Damned if I know," Al said. "But I'd trust Clayton with my life."

"I wonder how he knew where to find you," Fergie said, "and why he was looking for you in the first place."

"I suppose we can ask him all the questions we want once we get where we're going." Al kept an eye on his mirrors, but as far as he could tell, they weren't being followed.

Chapter Thirty

Over an hour and a half later, Clayton led them back a long lane through a marshy, woodsy shore's edge to a lake that looked as if it had been made for the sole purpose of raising mosquitoes.

"We're still in the county, aren't we?" Maury said. "Have you ever been here before?"

"Not in many a moon," Al said. "We found someone running a still here in the first year or two I was doing detecting work for the department. Later, a meth lab was in the same place, keeping pace with the times."

"I like a location with a romantic history," Bonnie said. She'd had to change the baby's diaper halfway through the trip. Fergie had cracked her window, and Tanner had tried to get up into the front seat.

"How's the shoulder, Al?" Maury asked while they were still riding behind the cloud of white dust the cruiser was kicking up from the gravel.

"Better. Almost good as new."

"Did you go to a therapist, get it worked on?"

"In a manner of speaking."

Fergie chuckled.

Al still wasn't remembering that stretch of time at the warehouse with particular fondness or amusement.

The cruiser ahead of him swung around a final curve in the lane through thicker woods on both sides. As the view opened, Al saw a recreational trailer, a big white one, the kind that took a truck with a fair amount of torque to haul it.

Clayton was already out of the cruiser by the time Al pulled up alongside. He got out of his rental car and looked around. It had been a pretty out-of-the-way spot back in the day, and it still was. There were few enough spots like it these days. He could catch a glimmer of the lake in the distance. He'd been on the water outside that spot before, on his boat, but he hadn't been back there on land in years.

The sheriff waved a hand along the trailer's length. "My getaway spot, where I come to think now and again."

"What are you thinking just now?"

"That you have a story to share, one that involves you needing a hideout."

"You'd be right about that," Fergie said. She turned to help Bonnie out of the back seat.

Maury moved closer to the trailer. "It has a full hookup: electric, water, sewage. At least we're not boondocking."

"That hookup was already in place out here, but I had it upgraded, and the water is filtered now. You won't have any complaints about that."

"You want us to live here? All of us." Maury eased around the trailer to peer out around its other side. He turned to look back at Clayton.

Tanner moved closer to sniff at Clayton's pants leg.

Al was thinking much the same thing. He knew trailers like that could be spacious, enough for a couple or a small family. *But for the four of us, along with a baby and a dog?* He had just been thinking that his regular home was going to seem especially crowded. *But this?*

"You'll find it cozy," Clayton said, "and safe. No one knows I have it. Other than the wife, that is. And she doesn't have to know someone is staying in it."

He went up the steps to unlock the door, took the key off his ring, and handed the key to Al. "For as long as you need it."

"Do you want to discuss any of this?" Al said.

"Give that a moment or two. You'll see why in a bit." Clayton led the way inside.

At one end of the interior, Al saw a double bed on the other side of a partition. His heart sank as Bonnie took the baby in to the bed and put him down on it. She was staking out that claim for herself and Maury. He looked the other direction and saw two bunk beds by the small bathroom on that end. It looked as though he and Fergie were going to be bunking it.

A couch and a breakfast nook with a table and seats filled the extended part of the trailer.

Maury moved to the kitchenette and opened the fridge door with his free arm. The only thing inside was a six-pack of Spaten Optimator, a doppelbock beer from Munich. The only other time Al had ever seen Clayton enjoy an alcoholic beverage, it had been that brand. Maury shrugged and closed the door.

Somehow, seeing Clayton's own favorite brew made the place seem more personal and their arrival more invasive.

Other than the beer, little else in the trailer made it seem heavily used. It could have been a motel room, a fairly new one.

"You and the missus don't get out here much, do you?" Al asked.

Clayton shrugged but seemed unfazed. He flipped a switch, and classical music piped through the trailer. Then he led the way back outside, pausing just long enough to extend the awning for a spot of shade. The music came out softly through outdoor speakers.

From a sideways door along the base of the trailer, he got out half a dozen folding lawn chairs. Al and Maury helped him set them up. They had just sat down in them, looking back toward the lane they'd used to come in, when Al heard the burble of a motorcycle engine coming their way.

"That'll be the company I'm expecting," Clayton said.

Al hadn't seen Clayton use his phone. He must have made the call from his car while on the way.

"It's probably better if no one from the department knows where we are or that we're alive," Al said.

"We'll touch on that in a moment as well." Clayton settled back in his chair and waited.

A Harley rolled around the corner into sight. The biker riding it wore black leathers with a black helmet and a visor so tinted Al couldn't make out the face. From the stocky, muscled body, he had a sinking feeling who he'd be looking at when the helmet came off.

"Why him?" Al asked Clayton.

"You'll see or, rather, hear."

The man pulled up, put the bike up on its kickstand, and turned off the motor. When he took off his helmet, Al sighed.

"It's Jaime Avila," Fergie said.

"In the flesh," Jaime agreed.

They had all met him and been through a lot together. Jaime was the head of the local ICE, the US Immigration and Customs Enforcement. Al's apprehension about what he was in the middle of ratcheted up a few notches.

He grinned at Al. "I heard you were dead."

Chapter Thirty-one

"**P**ull up a chair." Clayton waved to an empty lawn chair.

Jaime held up a finger. He hung his helmet on the bike's handlebars and tugged off his leather jacket. He draped that across the seat. Then he went past them, up the steps of the trailer, and went inside. He came out a moment later, holding a bottle of beer. Easing into the chair, he took out his belt knife, with its six-inch fixed blade. Holding the top of the bottle in one hand so the cap was flat with the top of his fist, he used the edge of the knife to pop off the top.

Maury licked his lips and glanced toward Bonnie. She shook her head. Al knew she couldn't drink while she was nursing a baby. Maury hung his head a half inch lower and looked like one of those sad clowns at the circus.

"And these two aren't even married yet," Al said to Jaime.

"But have a baby inside," Fergie said.

"Inside the trailer, you mean?" Jaime winked at Bonnie, whom he had always considered a muffin. He took a long pull from his beer.

"Tell him the word you used with me, Al," Clayton said.

"Do you mean the Nechelovecheskiye, the Nobodies?"

"That's the one."

"Interesting." Jaime nodded to himself. "You met these people, and you're alive?"

"No. I met these people, and for all practical purposes, I'm now officially dead."

"You can confirm their existence, that they're here?"

"Didn't you get anything from the bodies at the warehouse fire?" Al asked Clayton.

"That's just the thing, Al. There were no bodies."

"But I saw some. Several."

"Me too. I was there," Fergie said.

"Well, there weren't any bodies found after the fire was out," Clayton said. "A few shell casings. But no bodies."

"You're pretty sure of what you heard and what you saw?" Jaime took another sip from his beer.

"What did Aaron Masterson report?" Al asked. "He was there."

"We have nothing confirmed there at all. The FBI's position is that Agent Masterson is still in deep undercover." Jaime glanced toward Clayton.

"Has he revealed who he's found at the next level up?"

"Not yet. Not to the Bu. Not to us."

"Still early times, eh?"

"Say what you will, but we were in the thick of it and thought we were going to die." Fergie leaned forward in her chair.

"Yet you didn't." Clayton tilted his head a quarter inch to the right.

"We got lucky," Al said.

"Yeah, and got away," Fergie said.

"No one helped you?"

"We got no help of any kind from Aaron. That's for certain. He had quite a chuckle about tracking his way to these people first, in time to cozy up with them and get bought by them."

"That's how it looked to you?"

"That's how it was." Fergie was close to shouting.

Bonnie reached over and put a hand on her shoulder.

"Did you see anything you can remember on those alleged bodies you saw as you were getting out?" Jaime asked.

Al glanced at Fergie then back at Jaime. "I saw one large T over an S on one guy's arm."

"Then you know why Clayton called me in for this little chat."

"This is tied to the cartels somehow?"

"You know what the tat means, Al." Jaime lifted his bottle and tilted it back until it was empty. He eased the bottle to the ground beside his chair and let out a small burp.

"Texas Syndicate."

"And that means?"

"Ties to cartels and other nasties, like Los Zetas. It means drug trafficking, prostitution, extortion, gambling, and just about anything else they can get into. You think they're in this, tied up somehow to these Nechelovecheskiye?"

"More likely opposing teams," Jaime said. "What else did you hear that made you wonder a bit?"

"Aaron said something about Armenians."

Jaime and Clayton's eyes locked, then both swung back to Al at the same time.

"What is this whole mess? Just another arm of the Russian mafia?" Al asked.

"We have to be very careful talking about the Russian mafia in the area," Clayton said. "As you know, Al, we had that messy real-estate tangle where the investors accused a family with a Russian background of a Ponzi scheme and of being Russian mafia. Six years of court time later, the Russians were cleared."

"I'm not saying that's exactly who these guys are. They're just a scruffy lot willing to add child porn to their bag of tricks for revenue and equally willing to snuff out anyone who might expose them, even their own lower-level soldiers."

"But what about the ones who attacked them at the warehouse? Who were they?" Fergie turned to Clayton. "And why weren't there any bodies to recover that could confirm any of this?"

"By the time the first-response fire-department units and all the backup units were done putting out the fire, there was nothing but wood ash. Since they all have arson training, they're going over that as well, which seems likely. But no bodies, no hint of warring groups other than a few shell casings."

Jaime chuckled. "That does give new meaning to those Nechelovecheskiye, the Nobodies. Get it? No bodies."

Al frowned at him. "I tell you they're out there, and Aaron is in the midst of one of them."

"But what if he is truly undercover and just going along to make a case, the way he was with those child-porn photographers?" Clayton asked.

"Then he was going to let us die to keep from blowing his cover. Say what you will, but that doesn't mean I have to like him."

"You were a pretty good detective in your day, Al. Based on what you know, what do you think was going on out there?" Jaime tilted back in his chair.

"I'd be guessing, and Clayton will tell you I'm not fond of that."

"Give it a shot," Clayton said.

Al sighed. "This is all chalk on a board, mind you, but I'd say some new group that's part of a wide and lucrative porn network, possible human trafficking as well, has been working very secretively in this area, and the revenue stream is big enough to bring some other no-goods out from the woodwork. Based just on scraps I've heard and read, some Armenians tangled with cartel-connected gangs in California and got the worst of the deal. What if they have drifted this way and are working hand in hand with some other prison-originated paramilitary group, like the Texas Syndicate? The combined bunch might have made a hard, physical play for these Nobodies."

Jaime stood slowly and took out his wallet. He removed a ten-dollar bill and handed it to Clayton. "You were right. He's still sharp as a mother-in-law's straight razor."

"I'll throw in one more thing for free," Al said, "that probably wasn't in your little bet."

"What's that?" The grin was slipping off Clayton's face.

"That the reason we're meeting out here in the middle of bumfart nowhere is the same reason you can't let any of your regular staff know about us being alive."

"And what exactly is that?" At least Jaime was smiling.

Al turned to him. "It's because Clayton suspects he has a leak, and he still doesn't know yet just who that is."

Clayton leaned forward in his chair and rested his forearms on his knees. "I've got someone with a rifle, a thirty-ought-six, and another person, or possibly the same person with a knife, both still on the loose. I have someone, maybe that same someone but probably not, doing pro-style hits with a twenty-two to the eyes. Then I have this warehouse fire and possible gunfight with no bodies. All resulting from you poking around at a kiddie-porn ring."

"With some possible cartel connection," Jaime threw in.

"All of whom seem far more informed than we are just yet." Clayton looked at him then turned back to Al. "I think you and Fergie ought to bring us up to speed and tell us exactly what you've been through."

Chapter Thirty-two

Fergie and Al took turns telling everything just as it happened, except for the part involving the Bone Lady. Tanner sat between their chairs. More than once, Al wished Tanner had a voice so he could confirm some of the tale.

"You kind of left out one interesting bit," Jaime said when they were done.

"Yeah, how did you escape?" Maury said before Bonnie caught him in the lower ribs with her elbow.

Al and Fergie glanced at each other, but neither spoke.

"I have some ideas about that," Clayton said, "so we'll let it slide for the moment since we have no bodies, or a smoking gun... or knife."

"Those Texas Syndicate boys are trained paramilitaries," Jaime said. "They have good cleanup skills and could have carried out any dead, for either side. It's surprising you even found any shell casings at all."

Al pictured them hauling Stomper's bulky corpse out of the burning building. That must have taken more than two of them. He'd looked every bit of almost three hundred pounds of mostly muscle. He hadn't been stronger than a knife, though.

"Let me make a point about Special Agent Aaron Masterson, if I might." Clayton glanced up at the trailer door, perhaps wishing he'd brought out one of those doppelbock beers. "It's entirely possible that he isn't bent, that he was just acting a role to ingratiate himself with these Nobodies. That can and has happened with a Bu agent when a child-porn ring is the objective."

"I don't care if that son of a bitch is up for Oscar consideration. He was going to let us die." Fergie's tone made Tanner crouch lower and press tighter against Al's leg. "You know that his men tried to break into Al's place, and you have our unflinching account of him gloating to us about selling out. I can guarantee if I get within a foot of him at any point in the near future that you're going to have you one of those bodies you couldn't find."

"Now, now. Calm down." Clayton turned to Al. "Since Jaime is pretty current on all the cartels and their minions here in the states, maybe you can bring him up to speed on the last widespread push against child pornographers on this scale."

"I think I—" Jaime started.

"Let Al stretch that remarkable memory of his," Clayton said. "But keep the info dump as brief as you can, Al. All we want is a snapshot context here."

Al looked around at each of them. Maury and Bonnie looked more rapt than either Clayton or Jaime. They looked like kids eager for a ripping bedtime story.

"Just a few years back, there was a combined investigation that involved the FBI and Europol on both continents," Al said. "An enterprising fellow in Florida had organized a pedophile network he called Rob the Cradle. It was set up on the dark net, skirting legalities with robust encryption and anonymity software to mask the identities of the users, who could share photos and videos featuring child abuse."

"How come even I don't know about this dark net?" Maury asked.

"Be glad you don't," Clayton said. "It's also known as the dark web. But you were telling the story, Al."

"It's an overlay network," Al said, "that can receive data but doesn't appear on network lists or answer to pings or inquiries."

"How'd they ever crack it, then?" Bonnie asked. She was keeping one ear cocked toward the trailer in case Little Al woke and started crying. They'd tucked him in pretty well with a makeshift crib on the bed.

Al crossed his arms and leaned all the way back in his chair. "The FBI is always on the lookout for anything to do with child porn these days. All they needed was a whiff, and they were on it and able to get one of their own actively involved as a user. Next, they used malware to occupy the forum themselves, which let them track and identify all the users. The shifty part of all this was that they did all their hacking on the basis of a single warrant. Then they took over the network and ran the pedophile site themselves for several weeks. In the end, almost nine hundred pedophiles on both continents were arrested. And the founder of Rob the Cradle was caught and sentenced to thirty years in prison, where he's probably kept out of the population since he'd be roughed up for having short eyes if the others knew, and they usually do."

"This is the same way that Aaron is operating. If he's still a legit agent at all, which I strongly doubt. He's breaking the law. Plain and simple." Fergie's lip curl wasn't attractive to Al, but he agreed with her.

"How come we haven't heard more about this?" Maury asked

"Because some of the people who were investigated were too far up the power food chain: celebrities, politicians, and some of the richest global elitists you can imagine." Al caught Clayton's frown. "At least, that's the most widely held opinion about why so little has been done or actually accomplished."

Clayton stood and ran his hands down the tops of his uniform pants to straighten the legs. "So that leaves us with no active leads, no place to start, and a couple or three violent groups roaming around completely out of sight."

"And a probable rogue FBI agent in the mix," Al said.

Clayton winced. "Maybe. But Jaime and I have our work cut out for us. And by that, I mean just *us*. I want all of you to stay put. Do nothing."

Jaime stood and headed for the Harley.

"You want us to do *nothing*?" Fergie asked.

Clayton grinned back over his shoulder. "Relax. Enjoy the swampy air."

He climbed back into his cruiser and was soon kicking up another cloud of white dust as he headed slowly out the lane.

In a trailer full of four people, a baby, and a dog, Al didn't think relaxation was going to be an achievable objective. Besides, the restless itch to finish something he'd started was gnawing inside him.

Chapter Thirty-three

While the roiling cloud of white dust along the lane was still settling, the baby began to cry inside the trailer.

Bonnie jumped up from her chair and shot up the stairs and into the trailer. Maury gave Al a look as though he'd just swallowed gum he wasn't chewing and followed.

"My first thought was to send them off to Vegas, where they could get married in the bargain if they want." Al led Tanner up the steps. "But I suspect they'll be better off here."

"And as good as Maury's been about having a son, I'm not sure he's ready to slip on the ring just this week." Fergie chuckled.

They went inside, where Maury was helping change the baby. That in itself was a sight Al had never expected to see.

"We're going to have to stock this place with a few groceries," Al said.

"And diapers. In Germany, a beer like we have in the fridge is considered a food." Maury nodded toward the kitchen. "But since that's all we have..."

"I'll put together a list," Bonnie said. "We have some special needs, and I don't mean for Maury. Now, if you don't want to see me breast-feed the baby, you'd better go back outside."

"I'll stay and watch," Maury said.

"Get some paper and a pencil," Bonnie said.

"We're leaving Tanner with you guys—home protection and all that." Al held out a hand to keep the dog inside as he closed the door.

He and Fergie stood outside in a growing light breeze, waiting for the list.

In a few moments, Maury came outside and handed over Bonnie's grocery needs. He was holding an open bottle of beer in his sling hand and reached for it with his free hand.

Al glanced toward the trailer door. At least the baby wasn't crying at the moment. He looked at Maury's face. "No, you can't come with us. Stay here, and take some pictures of the baby or something."

Maury frowned. "Bonnie says I have an entirely different and twisted idea about what a selfie stick is."

Al shook his head as he turned and headed for the car.

?

When Al and Fergie came back into the trailer, carrying the first bags of groceries from the car, as well as new matching food and water bowls for Tanner, Maury sat on the couch, holding the baby with his good arm.

Maury held up a finger to his lips. He nodded toward the master bed, where Bonnie lay on her side, snoring lightly. "She was exhausted."

"Well, aren't you the regular papa in charge now," Fergie whispered.

She and Al quietly brought in all they'd bought at the grocery and stowed it in the small kitchen until the fridge fairly bulged with food. They put a pecan pie on the dinette table.

"Oh, she'll like that," Maury whispered. "Since she can't drink, she's had a real sweet tooth."

Fergie put a pot of water on so they could have coffee. Then she went to the couch to take the baby from Maury and give him a rest.

Although they spoke quietly, Bonnie soon stepped out from the master bedroom, such as it was. She stretched and yawned then held out her hands. Fergie handed her the baby.

Bonnie saw the pie. "Thanks for that."

Maury reached up with his free hand to rub at the shoulder of the arm in a sling.

"How's the shoulder?" Bonnie asked.

"Oh, just fine. Great. It's like I was hardly shot at all."

"Hard to believe anyone would want to shoot you. I mean these days since you're more settled down. Now, back a few years ago, with outraged husbands roaming the earth, I could see someone popping you then." Bonnie chuckled.

"That's part of what rubs my rhubarb," Al said. "There are loose ends here that don't fit at all, not the least bit."

"You mean like the thirty-ought-six?" Fergie asked.

"And the knife work that is supposed to point toward the Bone Lady."

"You don't think she's capable?"

"Oh, she is. But no. Though she may have motivation, I don't see means and opportunity. Aside from her not having a sound alibi for the time of Ardisson's death, she didn't do it. Her style would have been to say nothing to me in the first place and just go over then and slice him up like a honey-baked ham."

"And if the thirty-ought-six has nothing to do with these Nechelovecheskiye people," Fergie asked, "then who stands to gain from going around shooting at some of the people involved, including Maury?"

"Yeah," Al said. "Kyle Morris is the only one of those at the motel that night not killed, other than Aaron, and he's been moving around like a jumping bean, getting all kinds of fresh work."

"I'll bet all this exposure from the murder investigations surrounding him surely would put Kyle Morris in even greater demand." Maury grinned.

"What the devil are you talking about?"

"It's like that guy whose wife cut off his dingus with a kitchen knife, and it was reattached after some hunting. He got all kinds of job offers. Imagine an alleged wife-beater like that getting roles in porn flicks, and I heard he even got a job as door greeter at a Las Vegas whorehouse. Personally, he's nobody I'd care to shake hands with, but there you have it. Fame is fame."

Al looked at Fergie, whose eyebrows were arched all the way, but he chuckled. "Maury, you're a genius."

"Everybody says that, but nobody pays me the big bucks."

Al reached for his cell phone.

"I thought we were supposed to be dead," Fergie said.

"There's more to this mess that has to be untangled yet."

"And you're just the guy to do it?"

"Of course." He made a call. "Hello, Victor?"

"Yeah?"

"Do you know if any charges were filed at all on this Kyle Morris fellow?"

"How very odd of you to ask, Al. Are you clairvoyant? Do you have ESPN or something?"

"What are you talking about?"

"I just heard from Moose Tarleton. They're at the crime scene now."

"What crime scene?"

"The one at Kyle Morris's place. Someone canceled his ticket for the porn Oscars."

"With a boning knife?"

"Hey, what are you pulling here?"

"It was, wasn't it?"

"Yeah. You've got some explaining to do, though."

"I'm going to take a quick spin into town and go over there."

Victor sighed. "I'd better go too. I'm the deputy who helped the feds process that knife mess at E. Z. Ardisson's place."

?

As they got out of the car outside the building that, until that day, had been the residence of Kyle Morris, Fergie nudged Al's arm and pointed at an unmarked car in the line of those outside. "Looks like Lieutenant Strummers is in on this too. That should make it jolly fun."

An officer in uniform stopped them at the open door to Kyle's apartment. A voice inside called out, "It's okay. You can let those two in."

The body was still sprawled on the kitchen floor. The city ME was going over it, but he must have been nearly done. His assistant stood close, holding a body bag.

"What do you think, Al? Does the job look familiar?" Moose Tarleton stood over by the fridge, Strummers beside him with his arms folded on his chest.

Al nodded.

Victor Kahlon sat in a chair at the dinette table. "That's what I told them. This is a mirror image of the MO at Ardisson's home. We didn't get any prints there, and I doubt they get any here."

"It's good of you to come all the way to give us that much," Strummers said. He turned to Al. "Any ideas about this?"

"He was a loose end, one in on a filming session that took place in the county."

"Ah. Child porn, wasn't it? Do you think someone took him down because they thought he had short eyes?"

"That's entirely possible." Al looked around. "Do you mind if I have a quick look around?"

"What do you hope to find?"

"I'll tell you if I spot it."

"Might be a good idea," Victor said. "I'm beginning to think Al knows more than he's shared so far."

"Okay." Strummers turned to Moose. "But give him a pair of gloves and follow him around like you're his second skin."

"Nice to see you too," Fergie said.

"Hey, Fergie. I saw you there. I was just thinking hard," Lieutenant Strummers said.

"There's a lot to think about in all this," she admitted.

Al tugged on the gloves Moose got for him and started through the apartment, first hitting the obvious places that could hold an object the size he expected. He started with the closets. Victor and Fergie followed along, staying almost as close as Moose did to Al.

When Al crouched down to look under the bed, he said, "Ah, there it is. You'd better get it out, Moose."

The bulky city detective crouched down to look under the bed. "Well, I'll be damned." He reached far back in and came out with a rifle.

"My money's on it being a thirty-ought-six," Al said.

Moose looked closer. "Well, I'll be damned." He looked at Al, his eyes narrowing. "What made you think of this?"

"Just a hunch. Any chance you can run ballistics on it?"

"And match it against what?"

"The round that was fired and hit my brother," Al said.

"What did he have against your brother?"

"I think he was probably just shooting at the truck. He might've taken a shot at the FBI agent on this as well."

"And you think someone killed him over that, with a knife?"

"I won't be surprised if that doesn't have anything to do with it at all, except as it loops back to his involvement in child porn."

"I can't say you're making any of this clearer," Moose said.

"Can't be helped for the moment," Al said. "One more thing. Did you ever get a make on the rifle that popped those two Russians, including Ian Burkhov?"

"Yeah."

"Could it have come from an AR-15?"

Moose's mouth opened, but he didn't say anything.

"You're starting to spook us here, Al," Victor said.

"I was there, heard the sound of that gun. But I'd like to know more about the gun that shot my brother." He nodded toward the rifle Moose held. "And there's a good chance this is it."

"You're going to have to share more than that," Moose said.

"You saw those still photos from his career that line his front hallway, the ones intended to make any visitor consider him a movie star?"

Moose nodded.

"When Fergie and I visited Kyle's place earlier, the only picture we saw among them that was in any way personal was one of Kyle and what was probably his late father. They were wearing hunting clothes. So I figured Kyle might have inherited a rifle in the estate. I also mentioned heading to the hospital next while Fergie and I were still in the apartment, and then, *bam*, someone takes a shot there at my truck."

"Why go around shooting at people with it?" Victor asked.

"Maury's theory is that the rumors going around this particular film industry, spiced up with a heightened sense of danger, would get Kyle a lot more work, bring in more money. He told us his agent's phone was ringing off the hook."

"But you don't think that's why someone put a knife in him?" Moose asked.

"No. Not for the shooting with a rifle, anyway. He's just another esteemed member of that motel filming moment who got removed. Kyle won't be starring in any more porn films. That'll be a hit for the Viagra industry."

Victor shook his head. "Let's give Moose time to confirm what you suspect with ballistics. No need to stay around. Everyone knows where you live."

Al nodded. At least Clayton hadn't shared Al's whereabouts with anyone in the department.

He and Fergie headed for the door, getting a grunted farewell from Strummers as they went past the crew putting Kyle in the body bag.

When, an hour and a half later, they got back to the trailer, Bonnie and Maury were waiting. Al told them about Kyle and finding the rifle. Bonnie softly patted Maury's hurt shoulder.

"You think Kyle Morris is the one who shot me?" Maury said. "He's one of my heroes. I'm a fan. Why would he do that?"

"Maybe he wasn't aiming for you. More likely at me. Maybe he was just stirring things up to increase his own marquee value, like you said. At the very least, he was part of what was making a tangle of the logic it takes to figure out just what was going on here."

"It doesn't make him seem very bright," Maury said.

"I met the man," Fergie said. "If brains were leather, he wouldn't have enough to saddle a flea."

"And someone did him in with a knife." Maury shook his head. "Is that another piece that doesn't fit?"

"Oh, I have a hunch about that one. It gives us one more thing to do." Al started toward the door.

"You're heading out of here, aren't you?" Maury asked. "Can I come too?"

"No way. Stay here and heal."

Maury shrugged as best he could with one bum shoulder. "Chances are that before the day is done, you two will find some new way to halfway get yourselves killed. I guess I am getting too old for that sort of thing."

"Not to mention you have a child to raise now," Fergie said.

"And pay for somehow," Maury said. "Heaven knows how." He did manage a wave as Al and Fergie went back out the trailer's door.

?

The Bone Lady came into the living room. Gerta stood by the mantel of a fireplace that didn't look as though it had ever been used. She liked a good fire of an evening on a chilly day, though that part of Texas wasn't known for its chilly days.

Gerta had lifted down a giant pine cone that came from who knew where.

"Don' poke around in the man's house. He's kind enough to let us stay here while some folks may be looking for us at ours."

"How do you know he's kind?" Gerta put the pine cone back up next to a conch shell with a pink center.

"You'll learn about men in time. Some are good. Others not at all. The confusing ones are those in the middle who could go one way or the other when something comes along to tempt them."

"Tempts them to be good?"

"Rarely that, Gerta. Rarely that at all."

Chapter Thirty-four

By late afternoon, the Texas heat had picked up until Al could see wavy ripples of air rising from the dark asphalt as he pulled onto the edge of the lot where his new neighbor had been clearing the land. "Probably best if we aren't seen too close to the house, even with a different car."

He and Fergie hiked across to Al's house, staying as much as they could in the thick of the woods on the buffer lot keeping Austin's growing population from coming right to his door.

It felt odd to see the Bone Lady's car and his own truck parked out front and to knock at his own door.

She swung the door open and gave him a twisted grin. "Welcome to your own house."

"We'll just be a moment getting a few things."

"Take your time. Word on the street is you're both dead. Leastwise, no one's come looking for you yet."

"I guess that's a good thing." Al went to his gun safe and worked the combination. He ignored the long guns as he swung the door open. Instead, he reached for a black bag at the bottom of the safe. "Do you want anything left out for you to use? A shotgun maybe?" he asked the Bone Lady, who'd followed them into his bedroom.

"Naw. I can always find something in the kitchen to make do. Like I said, it's been as quiet around here as possible."

"Where's Gerta?" Fergie asked.

"She's down lying in the sun on your dock. Says staying here is like a trip to the beach. I'm afraid her tan is gonna to make her look even more like she's living up to her heritage. Do you two want anything to eat while you're here, in your own home?"

"We visited a grocery earlier and are pretty stocked up." Al didn't mention he'd stopped on the way there to pick up some of his usual stakeout food for the evening ahead. From a bottom drawer, he took out an envelope that held two thousand dollars in hundreds, his emergency mad money. That left one or two slightly larger envelopes still in there. If this spending kept up, and with the looming threat of hospital bills, even what he had might not be enough. He shrugged off that niggling thought and closed the bottom drawer. He put his spare Sig Sauer into the black bag and held up a Smith & Wesson revolver left over from his early days in the department. Fergie reached for it. He handed her a box of ammo.

"Going hunting?" the Bone Lady asked.

"In a manner of speaking," Al said.

"I would have dressed out some venison, but I know these deer around here are like pets to you."

"How do you know that?"

"Everyone knows that. It's part of what makes you you."

?

Al eased the rental car up the long lane with its lights out. He wore night-vision goggles he'd taken out of the black bag full of all manner of spyware gadgets.

Almost at the house, he backed the car into the copse of sumac and cedar he'd used every time, thick enough he could barely see out. He turned off the engine.

The house loomed dark and empty, not a light on anywhere.

"Doesn't look like anyone's home," Fergie said.

"Let's give it a while."

"What are you expecting?"

"You'll see."

They cracked their windows and let the night sounds come in from the darkness around them. Birds and insects chattered in low night murmurs. An owl sounded not too far from them. *Hoot. Hoot. Whooo.*

Wind rustled the leaves and limbs until they swept the sides and top of the car. Still, no lights came on in the house. The time stretched out long, like dark taffy being pulled oh so slowly.

They took turns, one using the binoculars awhile, the other the night-vision goggles, then switching.

"Really, Al?" Fergie whispered. She took off the night-vision goggles and lowered them. "We're watching an empty house here. Are you waiting for him to come home?"

"Not exactly. Give it a bit more."

They waited in near silence, except for the night sounds, for another hour. Al was moments away from reaching for the key to leave when he caught a faint crunch of gravel from a light, careful step. He lowered the binoculars and reached for the night-vision goggles.

Fergie started to whisper something. He held up a finger.

In the dim light from the stars and a slightly fatter moon, he could begin to make out a figure coming slowly up the lane, pausing to look around from time to time.

He took off the goggles and handed them to Fergie, who slipped them on.

"Oh," she gasped under her breath.

The figure paused.

Al reached out a hand to grip Fergie's forearm. She didn't say anything else.

The figure resumed its careful steps toward the house.

As soon as the figure slipped around to the back of the house, Fergie slipped closer to Al and whispered into his ear with her warm breath. "That was Sharah Hansson, and she's not wearing a uniform."

"Did you make out what she was carrying?"

"I did. It looked like a knife."

"A boning knife?"

"Could be."

They stayed quiet until Sharah came out of the house almost an hour later. Al had the binoculars at the time but could make out the brief dull silver flicker of the knife's blade, nothing fancy or chrome but the kind that might be found in a kitchen.

Sharah moved more quickly as she headed back out the long lane on foot.

Al gave her enough time to get all the way to the road. He started the car, left the lights off, and used the goggles to see his way out.

Near the end of the lane, he hung back until he saw her taillights flick on. She took off, and he followed from as far back as he could. When she turned at a corner, he risked tugging off the goggles and turning on his own lights.

"Do you think she's just going home?" Fergie asked.

"I hope not. Her steps leaving could have showed a little anger. Maybe she needs to talk with someone, a person she dare not reach out to digitally or by phone."

When Al saw her brake lights brighten quite a ways up the road, he pulled over. "We need to go by foot from here." He rummaged in his black bag then handed her the goggles.

Mosquitoes were out in great numbers and attacked them after only a few steps. The night noises were even more profound as they sought to walk on grass and weeds off the shoulder, in order to make the least sound.

A coyote howled. Far off, another answered it. Then a chorus of the voices from a litter of small pups joined in, practicing some of their first howls in unison.

Fergie stumbled. Al stopped at the scrape of gravel.

"I'm okay," she whispered. She gave him a gentle shove.

Al could make out the sign for a roadside rest stop ahead, lately only a spot for picnics, with no bathroom facilities. Two cars were pulled up by the trash barrels next to a steel picnic table.

Al used two fingers to indicate that Fergie should watch. He lowered himself to the ground and crawled. He could make out voices traveling through the quiet night air the way sound does across water.

"You said he'd be there."

"I said he *should* be. He'll come back."

Al recognized Sharah's voice. The other made him stop crawling for a second even though he'd had a pretty good hunch. The other voice belonged to Aaron Masterson.

They continued to speak in low tones. Al concentrated on crawling to the back bumper of the rental car he sought, the one Aaron had switched to instead of using one of the Bu's black SUVs.

Al reached into his pocket and took out the GPS tracker he'd gotten long ago at a spy-gear store. Even with his fingers bracing against the strong pull of the magnets, the gadget made a click as it fastened underneath the car. He might have imagined it, but the conversation seemed to stop for a moment before the low murmur of the voices started up again.

The crawl back up the road seemed to take twice as long. He had to scramble to take cover behind a low cluster of mesquite brush that managed to stab him a couple of times in the process. The lights of one vehicle swept by on the road. After it went by, he heard the other vehicle moving away in the other direction.

After a minute or so, he dared to stand upright to walk the rest of the way.

Fergie was climbing out of a ditch and pulling stretches of buffalo gourd off her shoulders.

"She was upset Grunderson wasn't where Aaron said he'd be," Al said.

"Well, I think we've uncovered the leak in Clayton's department. Do we follow her?"

"No, *him*. We know where to find her. Let's hope Aaron leads us somewhere even more interesting."

"How do you think a connection like this happened? Or should I say 'why'?"

"I think Aaron was trading inside information about how much the Bu knew, to Uncle Sergei. He'd have even more value if he also knew what the sheriff's department knew or didn't know," Al said.

"And she wanted to know the bad apples in the child-porn business. So he let her know about the ones who didn't matter to him anymore. He threw them under the bus, and she was the bus."

"Apparently, Grunderson has also reached that stage of obsolescence to Aaron. He's joined the group of dispensable targets. Sharah has ached to do something about him for a while, something horribly outside the normal range of justice and law enforcement."

"About her. Do you think... I mean the knife business?"

"We can't say for sure about that just yet. But it would sure account for one piece of this madcap puzzle that didn't fit."

"And the knife found at Ardisson's place?"

"Maybe she buys in bulk," Al said. "At the very least, she's a woman on a mission."

?

Maury opened the fridge and peered in. His eyes were drawn to the remaining four beers of what had once been a six-pack. He reached for a bottle of water instead. He turned to watch Bonnie holding the baby, who'd awakened them, to her chest, a soft pale-yellow blanket draped over so Maury wouldn't get stirred up to any wrong ideas.

He looked around the inside of the trailer. "I guess we could live in something like this."

"You mean if and when we get married."

"Yeah, that." He took a sip from the water.

"You're supposed to say, 'Sure, and that'll be real soon.' Haven't you looked at your copy of the script yet?"

"It's just that the idea is scary."

"Don't you think your brother—and Fergie, for that matter—aren't scared to the core of their bones every time they head out that door to face God knows what?"

Chapter Thirty-five

"What do you expect to find?" Fergie asked.

"I don't know for sure yet. I just have ideas at this point, a basket full of loose, unrelated ideas."

Al followed the blip on his cell-phone screen, giving it an occasional glance as he drove through the darkened night roads into a pretty secluded part of the county. Such places were getting harder to find, but one or two still existed.

Ahead, he could see the sign for an RV court, the Lazy Cactus.

"Kind of out in the middle of nowhere, isn't it?" Fergie asked.

"Yep, and with a 'No Vacancies' sign. That's odd way out here."

Al drove past and kept going, giving a quick glance to what he could see of the lot. All the RVs looked ready to roll. None had the flower beds or lawn bric-a-brac of some RV courts.

"Maybe that's how these guys keep moving around without being found," he said.

A quarter of a mile up the road, a parking lot on the right opened in front of a failed general store that had located badly and folded up years before. Al turned in and eased around to the back, where his rental car could be as hidden as possible.

He turned off the engine and let his eyes get used to the darkness. Fergie handed him his Sig Sauer. He could hear her checking over her own pistol.

"So you have a handle on who was muddling the scent with a rifle and probably even who was using a knife. You think that just leaves these Nechelovecheskiye guys in center court?"

"They and whoever wants in on their temporary piece of turf. It all comes down to money, in the end, and power with people like this."

"That must be what tempts Aaron Masterson."

"I can't speak for that dude. His head and mine don't work the same way."

"These guys he's sided with have some opposition, though, don't they?"

"It's ever thus when really big money's involved. You saw this in the city, and we saw a lot of it in the county. One group is always knocking heads with the others. It's like a gory game of King of the Hill. Any big sweep by law enforcement that works against one faction only strengthens another. It's hard to keep track of who's who without a scorecard. Tell you the truth, I wonder how even Jaime keeps track."

"But he does."

"He does indeed. According to him, the Texas Syndicate has lost ground in battles with groups like Tango Blast and the Mexican mafia. And 'ground' means revenue streams back to the cartels. They're probably seeking to step up their human trafficking as well as get into all existing revenue streams, including the elusive child-porn racket. That they are willing to work with Armenians who were run out of California, more by cartel-backed groups like MS-13 than law enforcement, means they are desperate, and that means more dangerous than ever."

"And they're the good guys?"

"There are no good guys here. Even some law-enforcement types get drawn in by this kind of cash."

"Like Aaron."

"Or go off on their own vigilante vendettas when the system doesn't seem to be working fast enough, or well enough, or know how to get nasty enough."

"Like Sharah."

Al nodded though he doubted she could see that in the dark. That was no problem, though. Being dark was good. The dark was going to be their friend.

"Let's go see whether Aaron's up to anything here or if the place is just filled with families and octogenarians vacationing," he said.

"All we're trying to do here is establish whether he's really in bed with these guys, if possible, and then get out, right?"

"Right."

"Then let's do this thing."

He turned off the dome light and climbed out of the car, stretching his shoulder and rubbing it. He wasn't back to one hundred percent, but he was a darned better sight off than he had been just a few days back, when he'd been beginning to feel his years.

They hiked behind the failed general store along an alley until it bled into an overgrown two-rut trail that went all the way to the edge of the RV court. Weeds with burrs and stickers scraped across their jeans. Mosquitoes rose from the moist, dark shadows to suck at their blood and leave itching welts. Clouds obscured most of the stars and what little moon there was so that they could barely see until they got closer to the RV court.

Al heard Fergie slap at a mosquito, a brisk crack of skin on skin. He froze in his steps and listened.

She leaned closer and whispered, "Are we having fun yet?"

He didn't have to remind her to be as quiet as she could. They were close enough to see lights on in one or two of the RVs, even though the time was nearly one in the morning. He felt welts growing on the backs of his hands and scratched at the itching. It would be like him to get West Nile virus out here.

Laughter broke out so close to where they were walking that Al froze midstep. Fergie did the same.

A couple of men were smoking outside one of the RVs only forty feet away. The wind had whisked the scent of their cigarettes in another direction, or Al might have had an earlier warning.

Fergie crouched low and skirted an RV to their left. He followed closely behind. Lights were on inside, but no one in there should have been able to look out into the darkness and see them creeping along.

The group of them stayed up late. The RVs all looked ready to roll. Perhaps they were heading to a new location before dawn. That would explain so many of them being up at that hour.

The two of them moved through the court from one shadow line to the next, scurrying across the open gravel in places. Al could hear voices off to his right. One sounded enough like Aaron's for him to tap Fergie and point to his right. He headed that way.

The voices grew loud enough for Al to make out the sounds but not the sense of words. Al peeked around the corner of an RV and saw Aaron and Uncle Sergei both sitting on folding chairs outside the door of an RV. On the small plastic table between them, a bottle of Stolichnaya stuck up like a Russian Kremlin guard between two tall shot glasses.

Aaron and Uncle Sergei were both laughing about something, and Al could almost make out the words. He looked at Fergie in the dim light. She shook her head, unable to make out the meaning of the words either.

Al toyed with the thought of just leaving while they could. He'd established in his mind that Aaron was in bed with these Nechelovecheskiye. He sure wanted to hear what was so funny, though.

He motioned to Fergie. The two of them crouched low and slunk toward a closer RV. Al paused at a gap across to that next RV that would be hidden to the two vodka drinkers but would leave Fergie and himself exposed from the back for a second or two.

In a burst, he shot across, with Fergie right behind him. He thought he'd made it fine until someone shouted.

"Hey!"

A man in the RV they'd just scurried from slid open a screen window and leaned out to point at them.

Aaron rose from his seat and yanked out that standard-issue Glock 22 of his. The sounds of big .40-caliber bullets ricocheting off the asphalt and sidewalks along the RVs were almost as loud as the shots themselves.

Someone, maybe Sergei, shouted, "Nyet! Nyet!"

Lights flicked on in several of the RVs that had been darkened. Men poured out of them, almost all of them armed. Al had wondered how many men were in the group. So far, he guessed forty or fifty were pouring out of the RVs, and they were all after Fergie and him. Since they were coming from all directions, Al wouldn't have bet much on their chances of getting away.

Chapter Thirty-six

Al was running flat out. Fergie, with her long legs, pulled out ahead of him. They tore around a corner, almost running into a group of men coming toward them. Whatever the first of them expected, it hadn't been a woman over six feet tall. His head tilted back to look up at her. She chopped at his neck with the edge of her hand. While he was still falling, she started toward the next one. The three of them turned and took off in the other direction, which added to the general confusion.

That was fine, but Al didn't think they could keep the pace up long. There were far too many stirred-up guys.

Shots broke out on one side of the action. Al couldn't imagine which of them had opened fire, and the bullets didn't seem to be coming their way. He saw the heads of the men turn in another direction. They called out to each other in several languages, but enough of them spoke in English for Al to figure out the Nechelovecheskiye were being attacked.

He hoped for some branch of law enforcement but didn't give that much credence, especially when he caught a glimpse of one group of men bursting in from one direction with guns firing. From another direction, more men were coming.

The men from the RVs took cover or fell.

Someone grabbed Al from behind. He spun and rammed his elbow into a face. He tripped another of the three of them and, breaking all rules of sportsmanship, kicked the man while he was down. The third lifted his AK-47 and as quickly fell forward, hit from behind by a bullet.

Shots were coming at them from several directions, Bullets slammed into the sides of RVs and into the people defending them. Al thought he heard the big hammering sound of a .50-caliber gun mixed in with the other rattles and pops. He could see no really safe place to stand or run.

Two more men ran toward them. Al calculated it would be only a matter of time before he and Fergie were grabbed, but a spray from an automatic weapon took out both men from behind. They tumbled to the ground midstep.

Al grabbed Fergie's arm and tugged her toward one of the RVs they could get under.

Someone else had the same idea, crawling in under the same RV from the other side. The face that turned to stare at Al belonged to Uncle Sergei. *So much for standing up tall and leading your men in battle.*

He held a pistol in his hand, which he swung toward them.

Al knew he couldn't get to his pistol in time, and Fergie's Smith & Wesson was still tucked in her belt.

Other faces appeared on the other side. In seconds, they would be dragged out or shot at where they were hiding.

This is the end.

The *whop whop* of a helicopter and the roar of its engine thrummed so close that the ground seemed to vibrate beneath Al. He heard new yells, panic in the voices.

"No. Wait. Don't shoot. We may need them."

Al looked behind him. Aaron was there, leaning down to look under the RV with his gun in hand as well. He grinned then waved to someone behind him.

Hands grabbed Al's ankles, and another must have done the same with Fergie's. They were dragged out into the open, the fireworks of a gun battle going on all around them. Rough hands took away their guns and cell phones and used nylon cable ties to fasten their wrists together behind them.

Sergei crawled out from under the RV and stepped close to Al. "Do you have a car?"

Al nodded.

"Where?"

Al looked at Fergie then nodded in the direction of the old general store. He sought to make sense of the expression on Aaron's face, which seemed a mix of cockiness and being in on an inside joke.

For the second time, Aaron had kept Sergei and his hodgepodge lot from killing them on the spot. But he'd also shot at them and had tried to burgle Al's home. Hard to tell on the face of it if he was playing a role to find his way up to the source of evil or if he was enjoying himself immensely and getting rich while doing so.

Men on both sides of Al held his arms while two others did the same for Fergie.

"Let's go," Sergei said.

They all crouched low while two other men with automatics went up on point to lay down cover.

Ahead, a group of what looked like mostly Texas Syndicate men had established control of the path ahead. One of them held the .50-caliber Barrett M82 rifle Al had heard barking earlier. They would have a devil of a time getting around those half-dozen heavily armed men.

As he was thinking that, he and Fergie were still being pushed forward with urgency. Shots came from all around them. Al wouldn't have been surprised if at any second any one of them would tumble to the ground.

Before the Texas Syndicate bunch ahead could turn and spot them, a larger number of men in black SWAT outfits, faces masked, along with other men in helmets and green combat uniforms, charged in from the left. The Syndicate men took off to the right with the men in black following closely, picking one or two off with every few steps.

Some of the men in black Al recognized as ICE, while the green uniforms were the sheriff department's SWAT bunch. Intent on the Syndicate men, they were off and out of sight by the time Sergei's entourage got to where they'd been.

"Let's go, go, go!" Aaron yelled to the others. "This is our window of opportunity."

Al ran and occasionally stumbled, the two men holding him dragging him to go faster. He was working out the chaos behind him in his head.

The Nechelovecheskiye had been attacked by what was likely a mix of Armenians and Texas Syndicate. Then strike teams from ICE and the sheriff's department had swept in. Jaime almost certainly hadn't known where the Nechelovecheskiye were hiding, so he must have found and followed the Texas Syndicate bunch.

He and Clayton had their heads together, so both might well have been there themselves, on the fringes somewhere or in the middle of the fighting, if he knew Jaime.

None of that seemed likely to do Al and Fergie any good. The distraction of the SWAT teams arriving had cleared the way, and they were both soon stumbling in the darkness along the same two-rut road they'd used to get to the RV court.

They came around to the back of the failed general store, where just enough light was shining to reveal the rental car. The man to Al's right dug in Al's pocket and came out with the keys.

Al was panting and sought to catch Fergie's eyes, but she was looking away or down, too discouraged to hope anything at that point.

The group slowed, too many to all get away in the car.

Sergei turned to the two prisoners. "I say we kill them both now." In his right hand, he held a Colt Woodsman, a .22-caliber semiautomatic pistol once favored by professional hit men. The gun gave Al an idea about just who had personally taken care of Trick Gibson and the Minskys.

Sergei raised the barrel of his pistol toward Al and Fergie.

Chapter Thirty-seven

"Wait. We may need them as hostages," Aaron said. "There could be roadblocks."

"I don't like it. I say kill them."

"No. We need them."

"Well, in the trunk then." Sergei lowered the gun in his hand.

That a hot-headed killer like Sergei would listen to Aaron gave Al a firm indication of how much he valued the agent, like one of his own men, a high-ranking one. He must be paying Aaron quite a bit, and the agent, in return, must have been supplying the kind of information and effort that kept Sergei as hidden as possible and able to move a step ahead of any law enforcement, usually. That might include what the sheriff's department knew, as well as the FBI, but Al didn't get the time he needed to ponder or get anything like a clear, firm picture of that.

He and Fergie were manhandled back to the rear of the rental. The men were strong, and their hands pinched like large coarse claws. One of the men popped the trunk open. It seemed like the open jaws of a whale.

They put Fergie in first. It took them a moment to fold all six feet of her in there.

"You know that Aaron here is an FBI agent, don't you?" Al asked Sergei.

"Yes." He glared at Al, probably still wishing he'd just shot him and left him there.

"Of course he knows," Aaron said. "It's what he paid for. Already paid. And handsomely. He gets an inside track on how much the Bu knows or is allowed to know. I get more money than I'd get in a lifetime working for the Bu. More money, certainly, than you ever made as a deputy detective."

"Let's go," Sergei snapped.

In the distance, the crackle of gunfire seemed to be fading, but the roar of the helicopter rose and fell as it swept back and forth across the scene with its beam of light spearing down.

The men holding Al jammed him into the trunk, not trying to be careful about whether his head bumped or being gentle in any way. The lid slammed closed, and in moments, the engine fired, and the car was rolling along.

He thought he'd be able to hear those up in the car talking, but they seemed in a quiet mood for the moment.

The air was stuffy, the trunk was darker inside than the night had been outside, and he kept rolling into Fergie with every hard turn or bump in the road, and the driver seemed to be steering for those.

"Ever think you're getting too old for this sort of thing?" Fergie asked.

He didn't reply. His first thought had been that he didn't expect to get any older. But he couldn't bring himself to say that.

Pressed up close to Fergie, and with none of the air conditioning in the front of the car, the trunk grew warmer and clammy. They continued to jostle around until he figured they would both be covered in bruises. Though in the end, that might not matter at all. He had thought about death several times over the years and had been almost as close before. He couldn't remember when he'd had less hope of avoiding the inevitable.

He tried to think of anything else but failed. He tried to doze off but was as untired as he'd ever been. Every nerve in his body seemed to be quietly screaming to itself. He bounced along, the side of his face abraded each time by the carpet lining the trunk. It was dark. Fergie had to be just as miserable, but she didn't say anything.

At first, he had hoped the car would be stopped by a roadblock, but that didn't happen.

For a while, he tried to keep track of every turn the car made so he could sort out where they were. Then the despair gnawing at him convinced him that knowing their location didn't matter. They were both going to die.

After a while, he could hear the men up front talking, perhaps one of them on a phone.

More miles jostled along. Al had way too much time to consider every aspect, every regret, and every brief flicker of joy in his life.

He tried to force himself to think of something else, anything. He tried fishing but couldn't even reclaim the thrill of a hungry bass's strike or the smell and taste of salt water from his trips to fish in the Gulf or off those islands in the Bahamas. He gave his brief mountain-climbing days a chance, or making love. *Nothing. Damn it.* He kept coming back to the moment and their almost-zero chances.

Al speculated for a stretch that perhaps Aaron wasn't saving them from anything by keeping Sergei from killing them. Maybe he was just stringing along the time out of some smug satisfaction in giving Al and Fergie time to think, to ruminate. Al began to harbor the not entirely new notion that he didn't care for Aaron very much.

"Well, I guess we won't get to see Maury and Bonnie get married," Fergie said, making no effort to whisper. She sounded as though she had been crying.

"No," he said. "I guess we won't."

?

Fergie twisted on her side, seeking any kind of relief from the tie biting into her wrists. She wished their arms had been left free. Not just because the tie hurt, which it did like dammit, but because she would like to have had her arms free to put around Al, or to feel him put his around her.

After a life of living pretty much on her own hook, she had come to the desire of wanting to spend her remaining days with this sweet lug of a man. Maybe that's what they were doing, and they just didn't have as many days or moments left as she had supposed.

She listened to every sound as the car rasped along down who-knew-what road, stopping occasionally or making turns.

At one brief stop, she heard a familiar sound, the relentless irritating chorus of cicadas. Whole scads of them were having a go at communicating.

Normally, their sound scraped at her every nerve, adding to her stress. Hearing them through the wall and in the dark of a closed trunk, she welcomed the sound. It was just about the only thing that said one important thing, that the two of them were still alive.

Chapter Thirty-eight

After what seemed hours but almost certainly wasn't, the car pulled over to the side of the road and idled. The men talked quietly among themselves, although another phone conversation may have taken place.

Sitting still caused the smell of engine exhaust to become more profound, until the trunk's air was thick with it. *That would be quite a joke on them if they opened the trunk in a spell to find us already dead.* Al's thought was another thing he didn't share with Fergie, who was coughing lightly.

After a time long enough for Al to seriously believe he was in the early stages of asphyxiation, with Fergie's breathing as labored as he'd ever heard it, a vehicle with a larger motor pulled up behind them. It could have been a bus or, more likely, an RV, perhaps one that had gotten away from that mess back there.

He thought he heard everyone get out of the car. That was followed by some loud bickering. At last, someone got back into the car, put the vehicle in gear, and pulled back onto the road.

The next long stretch of bouncing around in the trunk seemed to last forever. Maybe it was forever. At least the air cleared some when the car was moving.

The vehicle finally did slow and pull over onto what sounded like the gravel of a shoulder. Al heard the driver get out and his steps click around to the back. The trunk popped open and rose. Even in the dark of night, Al could make out Aaron Masterson. He no longer thought of him as Agent Masterson.

"Ladies first." Aaron reached in across Al to help Fergie out. The struggle of getting her feet out and then lowered onto the ground took a while. As soon as she was standing, he said, "Now you, Al. But let me caution you. If you try anything, she gets it. Pow! Am I clear?"

He used one arm to get Al turned. His other hand held a gun pointed at Fergie. He tugged at Al until he had his feet out of the trunk, then tugged more until Al slid out with his feet on the ground.

No vehicles were coming from either direction. Al sure would have welcomed a truck or car of any kind going by and seeing them tied and being held at gunpoint.

Aaron stepped in close behind Fergie, put one arm around her neck, and with the other, pointed the gun at the side of her head.

"You see, Al, I've noticed this weakness in you. You are like some damned knight of old when it comes to the ladies."

"Most people wouldn't consider that a weakness."

"Well, I do."

Al glanced around. They were by a dirt lane that led downward through stands of prickly-pear cactus. The trees on either side were huge and might well have been pecans, though he couldn't see their leaves in the dark. They could have been on a stretch along Nameless Road. If so, he knew about where they were. *Where we are going to die.*

Al had never been a prisoner of war before, but he began to sense how those people felt as he stumbled along in the dark down the dirt trail Aaron seemed to know. Aside from his hands being tied behind his back, he was aware that the muzzle of Aaron's gun stayed pressed to Fergie's temple. Al thought and looked for any opportunities, yet he found none that wouldn't harm Fergie. They were both going to die. He couldn't let go of that.

Night noises crowded them, from the nervous rustling of tree limbs to animals scurrying away as they plodded through the dark. Fergie stumbled, and Al wanted to help her, but Aaron held her upright with a tight grip on her neck. The muzzle of the gun never left her temple.

At last the trail opened to a flat stretch where the grass and weeds gave way to just dirt. Aaron turned Fergie around until they both faced Al.

This is it. This is the spot.

"Undo my hands, and have a go at me face-to-face if you're man enough," Al said.

"Oh, I don't think so. That sort of penny-ante machismo thing might work with a sheriff's department underling. This is no B movie. It's time you learned what professionals do."

"You're no professional. You're a self-absorbed scum of a traitorous excuse of a human being."

"Really? That's the best you've got? I want you to consider some irony here. Take a good look at this gun."

Al could see from where he stood that the one Aaron held was his own Sig Sauer. He stepped closer. Aaron took a step back.

"So this is supposed to look like a murder-suicide, is it?" Al asked. "I doubt you have the forensic training to make that happen. Have you thought about the powder-burn contact wounds you'll have to leave to make that credible? And what about GSR?"

"You stupid old fool. Or should I say 'bitter old man'? Don't you think I soaked up more at Quantico than you picked up in a career of your backwoods dabbling? I know every step of what I need to do. And come to that, I doubt forensics will matter much at all. Your bodies will be out here long enough the coyotes are sure to make a right mess of you." A bit of spittle ran down from the corner of his mouth, which Al could see, dim though the light was.

Aaron had begun to shout. *Good.*

"Age has nothing to do with it. A man with your lack of moral turpitude doesn't have the spine to pull this off. Sell your soul for a couple of bucks maybe, but not..."

"I've had it with you, old man." Aaron stepped forward and moved Al's gun barrel away from Fergie's temple to ram it hard up under Al's chin.

Al could feel the hand shaking, trembling harder as Aaron started to squeeze the trigger. Without a second's pause, Al slammed his head forward, smashing into Aaron's eye and cheekbone.

Aaron wobbled back a step from the head butt, the gun loose in his hand for a second. He let go of Fergie and started to step around her.

Al kicked as hard as he could, once again splitting the uprights of the upper vee of Aaron's legs. His boot connected hard, all the way to the pelvic bone, jarring Aaron, who crumpled to his knees.

Al kicked him again, in the stomach. When Aaron fell to one side, Al rushed in and kicked him again, in the head. His foot went all the way back for another kick when Fergie yelled.

"Al! Al! Stop it. He's out."

Al realized how hard he was breathing, panting. He would have killed the man. It was what he deserved. But he stopped.

Fergie lowered herself to the ground and scooted close to the fallen man so her tied hands could go through his pockets. "Where'd you learn that sort of stuff?"

His heart rate was slowly returning to normal. "The French call it *savate* or *boxe française*. Foot fighting."

"I meant the head butt."

"That's street survival one-oh-one."

"We're a heck of a ways from any street. But I'm glad you knew it."

She struggled back to her feet. "Turn around. I found his pocket knife."

He backed up to her and felt the binding around his wrists pop loose when she sawed through it. He rubbed at his wrists and took the knife from her. She turned her back to him and held out her bound wrists. He was careful not to nick her flesh. The moment her nylon tie split, she rubbed her wrists, which were bruised if not raw in a spot or two.

Al bent down and took back his own gun. He shoved it inside his belt at the small of his back. He handed Aaron's Glock to Fergie, who seemed glad to have it.

She bent to fish in Aaron's pockets and came out with the keys to the rental car. "We'll need these."

"Take his wallet if you like."

"No thanks. All his money is dirty, as are his credentials."

Al bent down and retrieved Aaron's cell phone. "Since they took ours. We may need to reach out to someone." He stood and looked down at Aaron, lying there as though sleeping peacefully, one side of his face already showing the beginning of a purple bruise.

Either of them could have popped him where he lay, finished him off, and he would have deserved it.

"Let's see if we can find some rope or wire. Hell, a coat hanger will do." Al started back toward the car.

"Another of those nylon ties would be nice," she said.

"No time to order some on the Internet."

They got all the way to the car, and Fergie paused for a minute to lean with her hands against it.

"You okay?"

"I've just had the Mick knocked out of me for a spell. I'll be fine."

They looked all through the car but found nothing they could use.

"We should just take him along in the trunk," Fergie said. "He would like that."

"It means carrying him all the way here."

"I'm okay with that if you are."

They trudged back along the dirt path until they came to where they'd left Aaron, but he was gone.

Chapter Thirty-nine

They looked all around for Aaron but found no place where he might have hidden.

"Probably took off at a run and is miles away by now," Al said. "We'd better get back to the car in case he thinks of that."

Aaron wasn't at the car when they got back to it. The doors were locked, and he probably knew that, aware he no longer had the keys.

"Long gone," Fergie agreed. "Maybe those coyotes he was talking about have caught up with him."

"One can hope," Al said. "Why don't you drive?"

"Okay." She opened the door and slid into the driver's seat, still rubbing her raw wrists.

Once he was in, she started the engine, turned on the lights, and pulled out onto the road. They had yet to figure out exactly where they were.

Al considered the possibility Aaron might leap out from beside the road to try to get into the car, but they were armed, and he wasn't. Still, Al watched the roadside closely for the first few miles.

"I have a pretty good idea what road we're on now," he said.

"Are we headed the right direction?"

"Doesn't matter. Anywhere else is better than where we just were."

"Got to agree. Sure feels better to be riding on seats compared to being stuffed in the trunk."

"You won't get any disagreement from me." Al rubbed at his wrists and, when she wasn't looking his way, his forehead. *That Aaron had sure had one bony head.* Al had done himself a little harm there, but it had been enough to get the upper hand. He would do it again any day, no matter what kind of headache and bruised forehead it gave him. He could figure Aaron for not counting on an old dude like Al still having a scrap of speed and fight left in him.

The phone he held in one hand made a noise.

Al looked at the screen. The text message had just a number and a question mark. He typed in a response, "Where are you?"

The answer came back right away. "You know."

He read it to Fergie.

"That doesn't tell us much."

"But I bet I know to whom it can mean something."

The sun was barely cracking the horizon, turning the sky to the east a lighter gray.

He punched in Meat Jenkins's number. The guy had to still be in bed.

"Wake up," Al murmured. He let it ring until Meat finally answered.

"Who is this?"

Al had forgotten the phone wasn't his. The caller ID had probably said it was Aaron Masterson calling if it said anything at all.

"Meat, it's me, Al Quinn."

"What the hell, Al?"

"If I give you a cell-phone number, can you work your magic and tell me where it is?"

"Probably. Let me get a pen."

"I'm not disturbing you, am I?"

"You know me. I'm up to my ears in geisha girls here."

Al heard Meat rustling around, probably getting something to write on as well.

"Okay. Fire away."

Al gave him the number.

"I'll need a minute or two. I'll call you back."

"On this phone, Meat. And call me first, okay?"

Fergie seemed as anxious as Al. She pulled the car over onto a wide patch of pale gravel so they were all the way off the road. Early as it was, only a few trucks and one car passed them from either direction. But such was his state of mind, Al watched each one carefully.

Fergie coughed delicately, still clearing out some of the car-exhaust fumes they'd inhaled during their time in the trunk.

The phone rang.

"Yeah, Meat?"

"It wasn't a piece of cake, which, by the way, I wouldn't mind right now if you're delivering, but I got it. Looks like it's at a bunch of warehouses off I-35 on Middledorf Road down in Hays County."

"Out of Clayton's jurisdiction. Good."

"Does this have anything to do with that big gunfight last night?"

"Maybe."

"I still gotta call him and let him know, and you know how he's gonna be."

"Yeah, like a bear being roused out of hibernation at this hour."

"Right."

"Better you than me. I'll get you a cake when next I see you." Al hung up.

"You think that's a good idea, enabling Meat's little food issue with a whole cake?"

"He's going to eat whether I have anything to do with it or not."

"I suppose so. Now what? Back to the bat cave?"

"No, Alfred. Road trip. We need to head south." He leaned over and took a look at the gas gauge. They were fine. "Do you know where Middledorf Road bleeds off I-35 down in Hays County?"

"Sure."

"Then head there."

?

They stopped once at a convenience store for gas, diet sodas, and some questionable prepackaged sandwiches from a display cooler. Al hoped the green in his sandwich was lettuce and not bologna.

Back in the car, they switched over, and Al drove the last leg. He was behind the wheel when they took the exit for Middledorf Road.

After they'd gone only a few miles, Fergie said, "I don't think you're going to have trouble finding the place."

Ahead, Al could see at least three large black vans off to the left, tucked in close near one of the warehouses in a row. More vans must have been around the other side. The area swarmed with men in black, each of which was labeled with three large letters: FBI.

"Well, so much for Clayton keeping this to himself."

"This is bigger than both of us," Fergie said.

Aside from the tactical team members in their black gear, several female agents were escorting young girls, each wrapped in a dark-blue blanket, toward a row of cars off to one side.

"Uh-oh," Fergie said. "Looks like someone has tumbled to the center of this porn or underage-girl thing."

"My money's on human trafficking as well."

"What makes you say that?"

"Her." Al pointed.

A woman in some of the same tactical gear stood off to one side, watching and supervising. She looked over and saw them, frowned, and headed their way.

Al rolled down his window, letting out all their nice air conditioning. "That's Special Agent Danielle Cassidy. She heads the human-trafficking outfit out of Houston, the main FBI office in Texas. She reports directly to Bryan C. Richards, the special agent in charge of the Houston FBI Field Office."

"What's up, Al?" Cassidy asked. "Just feeling a little nosy?"

"No. I was the one who let Clayton know about this place."

"Well, you thank him for me. This is going to be big. Very, very big. Not only are we getting about seventy underage girls clear from this mess, we're harvesting enough intel we may be able to crack the code of how these perv dealers and buyers communicate. This place seems to have been their last-ditch hub."

"Didn't Aaron Masterson share anything about this?"

"No one's heard from him for days."

"I'll bet someone's looking. Internal Affairs?"

"You know how that is. Even if I knew anything, I couldn't share that with the likes of you. Aren't you retired, anyway?"

"Not as much as I'd like to be."

"Well, nevertheless, get the hell out of here. We're going to be the rest of the day processing everything and everyone here."

"Does that include a guy called Uncle Sergei?"

"Just go, Al." She turned and started to walk away.

"Hey, wait a minute."

She turned back. "Now what?"

"You can have this." He held out the cell phone.

"What is it?" She came over and took it.

"It's Aaron's cell phone."

"And?"

"It's how I tumbled to this place." He waved a hand at all the activity going on.

"How'd you come to have it?"

"Let's just say I found it."

"Okay. We'll say that." She shook her head, turned, and started back toward all the hubbub.

?

As soon as their car was out of sight, just a slight roil of dust and grit where it had been, Cassidy turned back and walked over to the row of bodies the ME was still going through while her assistants were bringing out body bags.

She looked down at the one they called Sergei, though the file she had on him had half a dozen other names. He had gone down shooting, and the round that had gone through his skull just above one eye was probably the one that had done the job, though he had three clear hits to the body as well. She sure wished she could have spent even a few minutes talking with him. He might not have shared much, but she never knew.

Then she glanced down at the phone she still held in one hand. Aaron, Aaron, Aaron. She would sure have liked to talk to him too. Al Quinn had been right, though: so would Internal Affairs. She'd checked twice, and his body wasn't among those the ME's crew was going through.

Cassidy wandered back to watch sealed cases of files being hauled out of the building and loaded into a truck to be taken all the way to Houston for analysis. Maybe they could tell more of the slimy story than the dead Sergei would have willingly shared.

The blanket-wrapped young girls still being led outside and helped into waiting vans tugged at her more. She couldn't believe how many were there, and she knew many more were somewhere else. She didn't know if they had parents or friends or any kind of family waiting on them, or if they would ever be okay after what they'd been through. She just didn't know. She tried to choke back any emotion but felt her cheeks grow wet with tears.

"Agent Cassidy?"

She looked up to see an agent coming toward her. "Give me a minute or two, McCauley."

"Okay, I guess I..."

She turned around, and his footsteps went away. She didn't want anyone to see her that way. She had a reputation for being a pretty tough cookie, and she wanted to keep it that way.

In a minute, she took out a handkerchief and rubbed at her eyes.

It's not fair, dammit. It just isn't fair to all these girls.

Chapter Forty

The motorcycle arrived first, kicking up its tail of white dust from the gravel lane. Not all that far behind it came the cruiser.

By the time Clayton had gotten out of the sheriff's department vehicle, Jaime already had his Harley on its kickstand and was coming down the steps of the trailer, holding two of Clayton's beers.

Clayton shook his head. He was on duty. That sort of thing didn't matter as much to Jaime. He handed the extra beer to Maury, who sat in one of the lawn chairs outside the trailer. When Maury simply held the bottle, Jaime popped the top off his own with his knife and handed it to Maury, exchanging it for the unopened one, which he quickly cracked.

Clayton eased down into the empty chair next to Bonnie and Fergie. He leaned closer for a peek at the baby Bonnie held.

"I didn't see any formula when I was inside the fridge," Jaime said. "That kid must be getting the real stuff. That's got to be a sight worth seeing."

"Only private showings," Maury said.

Jaime grinned and took a pull on his bottle of beer.

"I thought we might all catch up on a few things," Clayton said.

"Must be something, for you to drive all the way out here," Fergie said.

"Not so very much, and I do know the way here." Clayton leaned back in his chair and looked around at them. Maury still wore a blue sling, a sign of his participation in recent events.

"Is there still a Bu agent unaccounted for?" Fergie asked.

"That's not my personal issue unless he shows up around here. The Bu hasn't exactly been chatty about him, except to ask to be notified right away if I come across him."

"He should be pretty easy to spot," Fergie said. "Just look for a bruise on his face about the size of Idaho."

Clayton glanced at the bruise in the middle of Al's forehead.

"Once again, you two are lucky to be alive," Jaime said.

"Oh, we're just brimming over with good luck." Al turned back to Clayton. "Why the visit?"

"Well, for one, Richards over in Houston passes along his thanks. You put a nice little package on his human-trafficking squad's plate."

Al nodded.

"It's what he does," Maury said. "Goes about spreading his goodness and cheer."

Clayton frowned.

"What can you tell me about any Armenians, Jaime?" Al looked at him.

"Well, they're probably the ones who put the Texas Syndicate boys wise to this Nechelovecheskiye bunch, that there was a serious revenue opportunity. But the TS, being cartel puppets at heart, didn't play nice for long and soon sent the Armenians packing, kicking them out the way the cartel lot in California did. They're somebody else's problem now."

Al glanced toward Clayton but added nothing.

"They were long gone by the time you stumbled onto the two approaching storm clouds," Jaime said. "Aaron probably played up the Armenians to the Bu folks up the food chain from himself because Armenians sound sexier, and just TS would be an ICE issue."

"So I was never close to any damned Armenians?"

"Nope. It was all TS that hit the warehouse in Travis County."

"And the RV court?" Fergie asked.

"Oh, we hit that, along with Clayton's tactical teams. We were following the TS lot, and they led us there."

"We had no idea you were there in the middle somehow," Clayton said. "Seems like you're always a step ahead and right in the middle. You could have said something."

"They took our cell phones when they took our guns," Fergie said.

"But you got away in the end."

"Thanks to Al for that," Fergie said. "I was starting to practice praying, something I haven't done since I was in pigtails."

"For my part, I'm not even sure yet if the Bu thinks he went dirty or was just really acting out the role of his cover," Jaime said.

Clayton nodded. "I had no way of knowing if his zeal was well-intentioned. The Bu, being the Bu, likes to tend to its own housekeeping, but his superiors must have had their niggling suspicions. It's why I wanted you to stay close to the man."

"Gee, thanks. It only almost got me killed, and Fergie with me."

"Almost is such a heavy word. Here you are, hale and hearty as ever."

"I don't know about hale. I'm starting to feel the creak or two of my years."

"It's never slowed you down before, and it didn't this time."

"What slowed me was the tangle of two other threads that only partially belong, the rifle and the knife action. They did more to throw me off than help in any way."

"Which reminds me. Victor wants to know where the Bone Lady is so he can question her. She's a person of interest at the least, our top suspect if you really want to know."

"Is this about her having flimsy or nonexistent alibis?"

"Just let Victor know if you see her. She's not been to her job for a few days, nor has she been home."

It would be utterly unlike Clayton to wink, but Al thought the corners of his grizzled old boss's mouth came darn close to lifting a fraction of an inch. He knew the Bone Lady was at Al's house, but he was cutting Al the slack to communicate on his own. Al took it for what it was: a sign of trust.

"I'll give him a call. I'd like to speak to Sharah Hansson, too."

"You'll have to wait on that. She called in sick today."

"Did she really?" Al glanced toward Fergie.

While the two trails of dust were still settling back to earth after Clayton and Jaime both left, Al turned to Fergie. "Get what you need from here, and we'll pick us up a couple of cell phones on the way."

"Where are we off to?"

"Another road trip," was all he said.

Chapter Forty-one

"You know, sometimes the world can seem not a very nice place," Gerta said.

Al glanced in his rearview mirror and caught a glimpse of her. The Bone Lady had been right. Lying in the sun on Al's fishing dock had given her a tan that really emphasized her Native American heritage: high cheekbones, the reddish skin tone, and those oh-so-penetrating dark eyes in one so young.

"Is this about losing your boyfriend?" Fergie asked.

"He wasn't a true boyfriend. He was someone I thought I knew and trusted, but that trust was misplaced. It turned out he was mixed up in something not good. Not good at all. I do hope Eliska is okay."

That was a bit of a conversational leap, but Al expected as much from a fifteen-year-old.

The Bone Lady sat on the other side of the back seat. She hadn't said seven words the whole trip.

Fergie glanced at Al from time to time, probably wondering why he'd picked up the mother and daughter at his house and insisted on bringing them along.

With only an occasional contemplative pause, the girl mostly bubbled along as Al drove the long haul from his house to Port Aransas. The variety of Texas scenery rolled by as they left Texas Hill Country for the flatter lands leading down to the Gulf Coast.

The metropolitan sprawl of San Antonio gave way to smaller towns that cluttered the sides of the road. They passed antique shops, windmills, old granaries turned into restaurants, and grazing longhorn cattle. Open fields and vast stretches of brown and green contrasted with the thick cedar and live-oak woods they'd left behind.

Al couldn't get over how lively and animated Gerta seemed, rapt at each new wonder and eager to go in and explore every time they stopped for food, gas, coffee, and a chance for Al and Fergie to stretch their legs.

He thought the Bone Lady seemed more serene and content now that her daughter was safe.

She moved closer to Al and Fergie in one convenience store while Gerta looked through the ice-cream bars in a frozen-foods case and finally selected one with caramel, nuts, and dark chocolate.

"Why Port Aransas?" the Bone Lady asked.

"When we were in Grunderson's house, we saw a picture of him and his daughter Eliska on the mantel. The wife had been cropped out and the place she'd been covered with matting," Fergie said.

The Bone Lady turned to Al with those dark, penetrating eyes of hers.

"Sharah was inside the house. We think she surely saw it too," he said.

"The pier, the boats, everything in the background screamed Port Aransas," Fergie said. "The family had a small getaway cottage there."

The Bone Lady nodded then went over to the checkout counter to pay for the things Gerta had picked out.

"Are you sure this is a good idea?" Fergie asked Al.

"I guess we'll have to wait and see."

"When this E. Z. Ardisson became your... friend, how did that work?" Fergie asked Gerta when they were rolling again. "Did he approach you or you him?"

All Gerta said was, "People make mistakes when they choose friends, sometimes."

"And that affected Eliska?" Fergie asked.

"Eliska was already affected. But, yes, I had regrets."

Al had always considered one's ability to see the big picture as a mark of maturity. Some people came to that sooner than others. Some never got there at all. But Gerta surely had the toolkit of experience to give her a boost in that direction.

All that aside, she still seemed a sparkling girl to Al. Seeing her smile and look about with eagerness made him think of all those young women—as young or younger—who were being led out of that warehouse by female FBI agents. He wondered how the rest of their lives would go, if their families would be happy and eager to embrace them again.

The Bone Lady settled back into a brooding thoughtfulness on the rest of the way down to the coast.

To her credit, Fergie did try to initiate a conversation with her now and again.

"Does anyone call you anything other than the Bone Lady?"

"Not anymore."

That ended that for the next few miles.

"Oh, look at all those goats," Gerta gushed. "See, they're climbing up on top of everything they can. Maybe they want to see as far away as they can."

Al glanced toward Fergie. She was looking toward the goat farm, but anything like emotion had washed from her face.

Port Aransas opened and blossomed like the coastal flower it was. As many fast-food joints and weather-beaten homes lined the road as scenes worth seeing. Al looked about for signs of heavy repair and damage. Hurricane Harvey had stomped right through the town, wrecking countless boats and making some houses look as if they'd been in a blender. Some flooding had occurred as well, but it hadn't been quite as bad as the floods that had put most of downtown Houston underwater.

Al had always loved the place and had done most of his recent coastal fishing out of the town. He had felt physically sick when he saw the photos and videos on the news. Like all coastal towns that faced the possibility of hurricanes, it had begun healing right away and was mostly back to the way he remembered, albeit with some new paint and some buildings built back up from the piles of rubble they had been for a spell.

Gerta cheered when she caught her first glimpse of the salt water.

Al knew the town well enough to head right for the street he wanted. Not being near the water had paid off, though Grunderson had to drive to the gulf from farther out. Most of the houses near his part of town hadn't been flooded. A few had had their roofs torn off and trees knocked over, but that had been mostly repaired except for one or two that still needed some work. Grunderson's place wasn't one of those. Perhaps, as an architect, he'd taken measures to ensure it was solid. Sure enough, the eaves were closed off with a slant of wood that wouldn't let the wind get under and pull the roof upward.

The cottage was small but made of sturdy red brick, and the white storm shutters looked like the kind that really worked. A house farther up the street hadn't fared as well. Its roof was still partially missing, and only one short stretch of what had been a picket fence around the yard remained. Perhaps Grunderson had also done some fixing up on his as well. The place practically sparkled, compared to some other homes the same size Al had seen.

Grunderson's BMW was in the drive, another car parked behind it, Sharah's.

"We're in time," Fergie said.

"Almost in time." Al pulled over behind the second car as the front door burst open.

Grunderson came running out, wearing only boxer shorts that had been so hastily pulled on they were backward, which wasn't helping his running.

Behind him, the much-younger Sharah Hansson came tearing along, gaining on him and carrying a long knife in one hand. She wore jeans, red boots, and a white blouse. Her face was twisted into as much rage as Al had ever seen on any face. *Maniacal.*

Al popped his door open and took off running. Fergie was usually faster but had gotten a second or two of a slower start. Whizzing past both of them came the Bone Lady.

Man, she can flat-out run. A regular Jesse Owens.

Sharah caught up with Grunderson, grabbed an ankle, flipped him to the ground, and pounced on him.

Al glanced toward the doorway of the small red-brick cottage with white shutters. Eliska stood cowering at the doorway, wrapped only in a sheet. Al suspected she was otherwise naked.

They were never going to get to Grunderson in time.

Sharah stood up over the body, blood already pouring out of the fallen man. Too late for him. At the doorway Eliska's mouth was open wide in a silent scream.

Sharah looked up and saw them coming. She was still panting hard. She stood, raised the bloody knife, and rushed toward her attackers.

The Bone Lady was far ahead of Fergie then Al, with Al holding one hand up to his lungs.

As Sharah charged, the Bone Lady dipped low and came up underneath, grabbing Sharah's wrist and twisting. With no knife in her own hand, she was free to put all her own momentum and torque into a throw that lifted Sharah up off the ground, bending and screaming as she sailed through the air. She came down with a jarring bang and a clear pop. The knife fell from her hand, and the arm looked twisted into an impossible angle. Sharah screamed again.

The Bone Lady stood over her, keeping her pressed to the ground with one boot. She signaled to Gerta, who rushed toward the cottage to embrace her friend and pull her inside.

"I see why you brought the Bone Lady along now," Fergie said.

"If you don't mind," Al panted, "could you get the handcuffs I brought along out of the glove box while I call the local cops?"

"Sure, sure," Fergie said. "Man, that Bone Lady is something."

"Plus, she had motivation. Sharah was trying to lay the blame on her with all this knife business."

Sharah stayed on the ground, the Bone Lady's foot on her while she clutched at her broken wrist with the other hand. She sobbed and sobbed, unable to stop. "That man was a monster. A monster. Don't you understand? I caught him in the very act."

Al was going to say that sometimes to deal with a monster, you became a monster. But he kept that to himself.

Fergie was coming back across the patchy half-brown lawn, holding the handcuffs.

In the distance, Al could hear a siren approaching. He could look forward to a not-altogether-comfortable phone chat with Clayton, too.

But, what the hell? It hasn't been that bad of a day, all around.

Chapter Forty-two

"I suppose I do owe you one," Clayton said. He stood beside Al and watched a county worker ease a backhoe down off the back of a truck.

"You don't have to be here personally," Al said.

Fergie nudged him on his low ribs with her elbow.

Clayton's big head turned slowly to Al, who didn't know what to make of the expression. "Through the years, I have come to enjoy seeing how your educated hunches turn out... just as much when they come up a bust as when they succeed."

Al looked around at the empty kennels. The Happy Daze site sure had a different feel without the hysterical barking of dogs and the hearty ammonia aroma of over a hundred cats. Myra Henningdale had told him she had already placed a couple of the dogs. She'd not had room to take on any of the cats, but the other pet shelters had all pitched in to help with them.

"You do know that Aaron Masterson and his FBI colleagues went over this place. When the Bu searches, they usually turn over every stone," Clayton said.

"But Aaron spearheaded that search, which took place before some people were willing to believe he was up to his ear bones in this mess and on the wrong side."

"His bosses were just as surprised as I was. His record was pretty darn good before this."

"But there has to be a massive amount of loose cash floating around in an operation that needs several locations of varied sorts to launder its revenues," Fergie said. "And say what you will about the Bu, the first thing out of any agent's mouth isn't about the swell retirement plan."

"It's enough," Clayton said, "if one isn't greedy."

"And there," Al said, "you have the rub."

"You know, Sharah spilled everything. She was hoping to cop a plea, get the death penalty off the table." Clayton stayed focused on his men fixing to go to work on the slab.

"I thought her initial stance was that she ought to just be set free, that she was doing the world some good," Fergie said.

"I dissuaded her from that silliness. You all were witnesses to her killing Grunderson, and she admitted to doing the same to E. Z. Ardisson, as well as that porn star Kyle Morris. She was hoping your pal the Bone Lady would get the blame. Everything sure pointed toward your Native American with a knife."

"And the business with Aaron?" Fergie asked.

"He came to her first, maybe caught something in his first interaction with her. The deal was that he got information about anything we might know in the department, and in exchange, he pointed her toward abusers and the child-porn ring once they were no use to him. He knew what she would do."

"But he never said anything to us."

"Neither did she to us, and that's where she put the starch in my shorts. I don't like betrayal or anyone being disloyal... ever. From anyone, about anything."

Victor Kahlon stood with two other deputies over by the slab. A worker with a jackhammer began to pound away at its surface.

"Seems a shame to tear up the newest slab on the lot."

"Its newness is what makes it the one to check."

"I hear you. I okayed getting the warrant, didn't I?"

"Reluctantly."

"You're damned right, reluctantly."

"You remember our bet?" Al asked.

"I do," Clayton grumbled. "I attend your brother's wedding. Damnedest thing, a man a year older than you having a child."

"Yeah," Fergie said. "Condoms might be an appropriate wedding gift."

"I believe he has a wedding registry at the pharmacy," Al said.

"I'd hate to see that list," Clayton said.

Victor looked up from where the jackhammer operator was making all the noise anyone could want. He waved at Al and Fergie, who waved back. Clayton stood John Wayne tall with his arms folded on his chest, the brim of his hat putting most of his face in shadow.

The jackhammer operator stepped back, and the backhoe operator moved his machine close and clawed away some of the shattered slab. The big yellow machine backed away, and the jackhammer started up again.

Fergie leaned closer to Al. "I thought it was noisy with the dogs here, but there's enough racket now for World War Seven to be going on."

Al nodded. He looked at Clayton, and his frown made Al smile.

Watching someone build a house was mildly fun for Al, as was watching anyone else work other than himself. But watching a crew doing the opposite, destruction, would have been hard at any other time. Instead, he felt a tingle of excitement, one clearly not being shared by Clayton. In a twisted way, that also made the exercise more fun.

Twenty minutes into the process, the backhoe pulled back a large piece of the slab. The jackhammer operator stepped forward then backed away, putting down his tool. He waved to Victor.

The detective rushed over to the spot and waved his arms. He turned toward Clayton and waved for him to come over.

"What fresh new hell is this?" Clayton grumbled.

Al and Fergie followed along.

Victor stepped away, and Al could see several bundles of hundred-dollar bills shrink-wrapped in clear plastic.

"Zow," Fergie said. "How much do you think is there?"

"Over a million, anyway. Easily that," Victor said.

"Well, we're not going to count it." Clayton looked at Al and shook his head. "Sometimes, I forget just how damned clever you are."

"He has his days," Fergie said.

Clayton took out his cell phone. "Yeah, can you patch me through to the agent in charge? This is Sheriff Clayton."

He put his hand over the phone while he waited. "This is going to get his hair standing on end. Wish I could be there to see that."

?

High in a stand of mountain cedar and mesquite trees, the limbs parted, and a face peeked through, just enough to see without being seen.

The deputies had formed a perimeter around the stash of money. He could see no way he was going to get anywhere near it now.

Damn. Damn. Damn.

He let the limbs ease back together and turned to head back toward the road where he'd left the new rental.

Inside, he boiled. Everything he had ever wanted was gone. Everything.

He was far enough away that a little noise wouldn't matter. He kicked at every bush, shrub, and low-hanging limb the rest of the way out.

Chapter Forty-three

Plain and simple, the wedding had to be the oddest one Al had ever been a part of, even though it was taking place in his own living room.

Harley Struthers, Al's new neighbor-to-be, had turned out to be a lay preacher. He'd performed the service, all the way up to the "I do" from each. Al had felt as awkward as he ever had at being best man, though Fergie seemed to get quite a hoot out of being maid of honor. Little Al was honorary ring bearer though he was tucked in a crib to one side and was sucking on a pacifier as if it held rum. Tanner wore a collar of flowers that Bonnie had put together and thought looked cute, though Tanner could have as easily been wearing one of those plastic cones of shame, from his expression.

Gerta was the real flower girl, and she beamed at the chance to wear the new dress Bonnie had provided. The Bone Lady couldn't have looked less sinister, for a few rare moments. Once or twice, she darn near smiled.

While the couple showed off their rings and moved toward the table holding the wedding cake, Clayton rose from his folding chair and eased closer to Al. Relations between him and Al had been limited until the present, given all the scrambling around Clayton had had to do with all the agencies, the other departments, and the federal judge who'd issued the warrant on Aaron Masterson.

He learned closer to Al and whispered, "You know, Aaron never did turn in that encrypted information you and Fergie found. I asked his boss about it in person and got one of the blankest looks I've ever seen."

"I figured it was a way for Grunderson to communicate about child porn as a customer," Al said. "Not turning it in was part of what he was doing for Sergei."

"And those two poor saps you tracked down, one from the coffee shop, were killed to keep them from ratting out Uncle Sergei to the Chechens."

"The Chechens?"

"From Brooklyn."

"How were they involved?"

"Turns out Uncle Sergei used to work with them, be one of them before he branched out on his own in some enterprises even those self-proclaimed outlaw heroes didn't want to touch, like child porn."

"So there was no connection up and above Sergei?"

"Nope. He was the end of that trail. Aaron should have just sent up the flare and stepped aside. He didn't."

"You think he was the one who put the finger on the Minskys, got them killed by Sergei?"

"Yeah. I don't think he took a twenty-two and did the job himself, or he would have kept the money the Minskys had stored behind that wall. That was all Sergei. The feds uncovered several million in cash during that raid down in Hays County."

"And now Aaron is in the wind. They really haven't an idea about where to find him?"

"No. But the Bu now has his money, too. From the intel they got from Cassidy's raid, they definitely tied the money under the slab to Aaron. *When* it was stored there also gave them a precise timetable for when Aaron, along with all the information and protection he could provide, was bought and paid for by Sergei. Storing a lump like that isn't as easy as the Swiss banks and Cayman Island accounts, so Aaron had to do something with it. I figure what he got came from that being laundered through the pet shelter. He probably thought up pouring the slab over it, knowing it would be okay there until he could get back to it. Too bad for him it wasn't. Two-and-a-half million is a tidy sum, kind of hard to hide altogether."

"That was the price of his soul."

"It's a fair amount of money to someone on a special agent's salary."

"That must have put Aaron into a right snit," Al said. "It was all about money with him."

"It was what Sergei was willing to pay for complete protection and immunity from the FBI, something Aaron wasn't able to deliver, as it turned out."

"Ahem." Maury led Bonnie over to stand behind the table holding the wedding cake.

She wore a white wedding dress, which Maury had kidded her about, and she had fired back that he sure couldn't justify wearing white.

"I want to announce that, with a baby and all, I have worried about expenses, especially after both of us spent recent vacation days at the hospital, so I have become gainfully employed," Maury said.

He gave the small crowd a moment or two of hubbub chatter about that. "Hermina Vanderhausen, administrator at the hospital and known affectionately to her staff as The Hammer, has offered me a job as safety consultant at the hospital as part of their risk-management program, to offset growing massive insurance premiums. I accepted. She has also agreed, as a sort of signing bonus, to clear Bonnie's and my hospital bills."

"So you have a job and no debt?" Fergie said.

"Yeah." Maury sighed. "A job. At my age, too. But I guess it's doing something I get a kick out of, not to mention satisfaction, and Bonnie will be working there, too."

"They have a first-rate day-care program that should help us by taking care of Little Al while we work."

"Hey, maybe I'll get to go fishing again," Al said.

He caught a look from Fergie as she came to get champagne for everyone. That could have meant anything, from admonition to a promise of helping him fill some of that time alone.

Al stood beside the table holding the modest two-tier white cake, three bottles of champagne, and two rows of stemmed glasses. He waited until Fergie had poured everyone a glass before clearing his throat for what was going to be one of the shortest best-man toasts in history.

The front door crashed open, thrown as hard against the wall as possible. Tanner leaped up, growling. Aaron Masterson rushed into the room—his face half purple from a huge bruise that nearly closed one eye, and with white gauze taped over his left ear. His snarl of rage and his finger resting on the mini trigger and main trigger of a Glock 22 meant he hadn't come to talk in his usual windy way but had come to shoot and kill.

Tanner started in a rush across the room, snarling and growling. But he was going to be too late. Clayton was reaching for his off-duty piece in his boot, but he was also going to be way too late.

Al reached to the table, skipping over the serving spade to grab the wedding-cake knife. His arm came up in a lightning fluid motion, and with a snap of the wrist, he sent the blade flying.

Aaron stopped midstep, his eyes growing wide. He seemed to want to speak but was unable. His left hand started to reach up for the knife handle sticking out of the middle of his throat. He fell forward with a thump.

Clayton bent down to put his fingers to Aaron's throat. He looked up at Al and shook his head. Then he reached for his cell phone to call his department.

"I couldn't have done better myself," the Bone Lady said. She bent closer to look down at Aaron. Al saw the first bona fide grin he'd ever seen from her, though it chilled him more than encouraged him.

She shook her head. "Though I think we'll probably need to use another knife on the cake."

Dear Reader,

We hope you enjoyed *A Shot in the Texas Dark*, by Russ Hall. Please consider leaving a review on your favorite book site.

Visit our website[1] to sign up for the Red Adept Publishing Newsletter to be notified of future releases.

Other Books by Russ Hall

Suspense/Thrillers

To Hell and Gone in Texas (An Al Quinn novel)

A Turtle Roars in Texas (An Al Quinn novel)

Throw the Texas Dog a Bone (An Al Quinn novel)

Island

Wildcat Did Growl

Talon's Grip

World Gone Wrong

Mysteries

Black Like Blood (An Esbeth Walters Novel)

The Blue-Eyed Indian

Bones of the Rain (A Blue-Eyed Indian Novel)

Goodbye, She Lied (An Esbeth Walters Novel)

No Murder Before its Time (An Esbeth Walters Novel)

Private Prodigy Eye (Three Sylvie Thomas and Adam Clay novels)

South Austin Vampire (A Blue-Eyed Indian Novel)

The Hairy Potter, and Other Al Quinn Mystery Stories

Westerns

Bent Red Moon

Bullets in the Wind

Three-Legged Horse (A Justin Bodean Western Novel)

Keep the Bullets Flying

Buffalo Skull (A Justin Bodean Western Novel)

Young Adult Sci-Fi

Inside Jupiter

About the Author

R uss Hall has had more than twenty-five books published: mysteries, thrillers, westerns, poetry, and nonfiction books, as well as numerous short stories and articles. For many years, he was an editor for major publishing companies, ranging from Harper & Row and Simon & Schuster to Pearson. Now, he lives by a lake in Texas hill country near Austin.

In 1996, he won the Nancy Pickard Mystery Fiction Award for short fiction. In 2011, he was given the Sage Award by The Barbara Burnett Smith Mentoring Authors Foundation—an award for the author who demonstrates an outstanding spirit of service, sharing, and leading others in the mystery-writing community. In 2014, he won first place in the Austin International Poetry Festival. The Writers' League of Texas awarded *To Hell and Gone in Texas* its 2015 Fiction Discovery Prize.

www.ingramcontent.com/pod-product-compliance
Lightning Source LLC
Chambersburg PA
CBHW031122020426
42333CB00012B/189